S0-IME-004

An Ifugao Notebook

This photograph was taken in October 1962 from the top of the trail that leads down to Baynīnan. The long thatched roof is our field lab and the pointed roof to its right is our house.

An Ifugao Notebook

Jean M. Conklin

2002

ISBN: 1-4033-4916-9 (e-book)
ISBN: 1-4033-4917-7 (Paperback)

This book is printed on acid free paper.

1stBooks - rev. 09/28/04

Many happy memories

for

my family

Contents

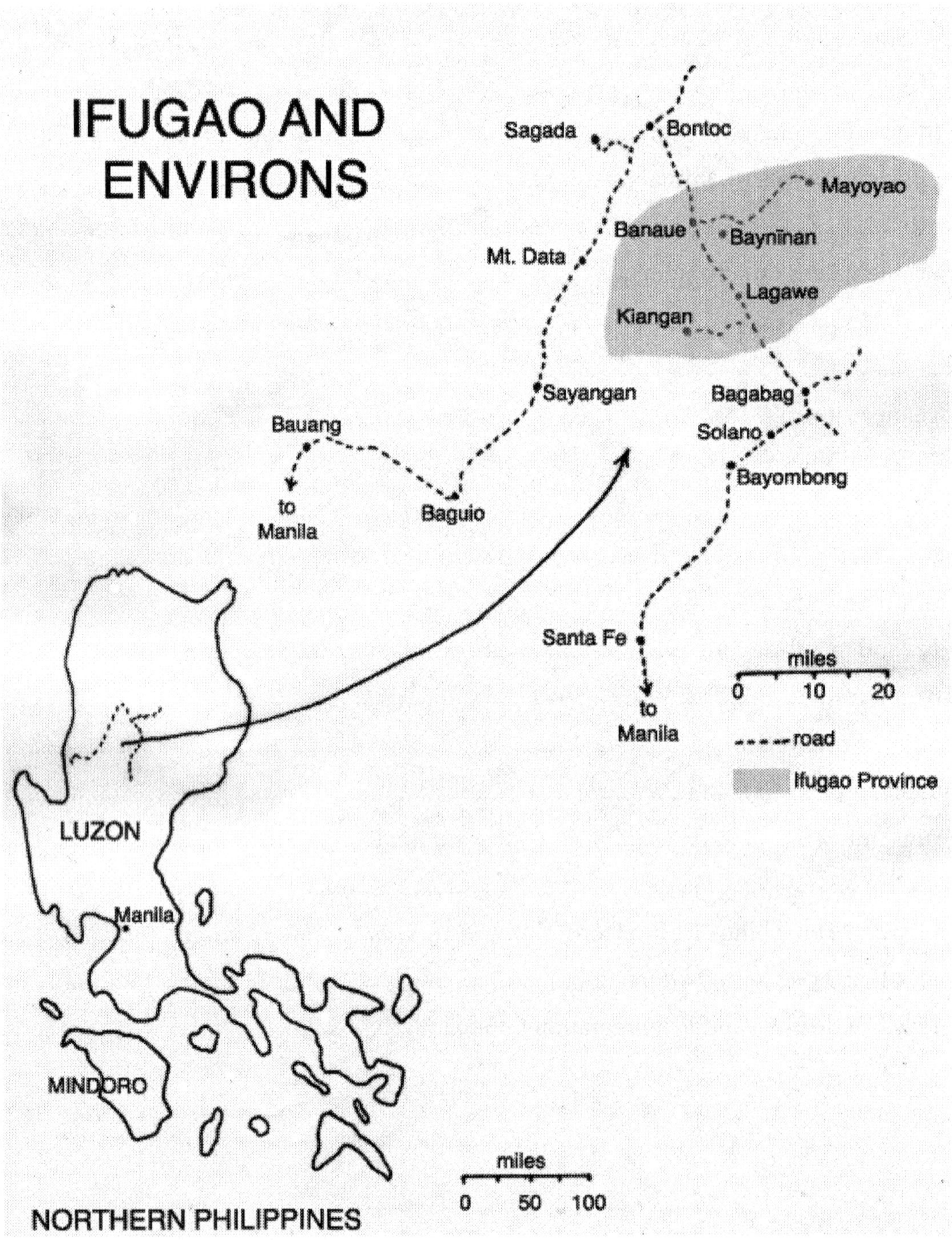
IFUGAO AND ENVIRONS
Sagada
Bontoc
Mayoyao
Banaue
Baynīnan
Mt. Data
Lagawe
Kiangan
Sayangan
Bagabag
Bauang
Solano
Bayombong
to Manila
Baguio
Santa Fe
miles
0 10 20
to Manila
road
Ifugao Province
LUZON
Manila
MINDORO
miles
0 50 100
NORTHERN PHILIPPINES

Introduction

From 1945 until the present, 2002, my husband, Harold C. Conklin, who is currently Professor Emeritus of Anthropology at Yale University, has been actively engaged in field research in the Philippines. His first visit to the mountains of northwestern Luzon, the locale of the following narrative, was in 1946 as a G.I. on a weekend pass while stationed in the Manila area. After his discharge he completed his undergraduate work at the University of California, Berkeley, and went on to get a Ph.D. in anthropology at Yale. His first teaching position was at Columbia University where he remained for eight years before returning to Yale.

His early work in the Philippines was with the Hanunóo, a group of swidden farmers living in the mountains of Mindoro. In addition to studying their agricultural practices and use of plants, his interests covered language, color categorization, music, rituals, and life in general.

In the early 60's, while continuing his interest in rice cultivation, Hal shifted his focus to the Ifugao in Northern Luzon, long known for their extensive rice terraces. He chose the agricultural district of Baynīnan in the Banaue area as his research site for a number of reasons. The district is large enough to be representative of the area yet not so large as to make comprehensive data-gathering an impossible task. As for location, the steep, often slippery hike down to the Baynīnan settlements discourages most tourists from trying to hike in, yet a sure-footed local resident can easily make the round trip from Baynīnan to Banaue within a day for mail and supplies.

Most importantly, Ottēngan ('oat-TEH-ngan), the ritual head of Baynīnan, was willing to take a chance on having a family of total strangers as neighbors. Little did he know at the time that the personal friendships established then would endure for decades and result in literally putting the community on the map. Every resident of Baynīnan contributed in one way or another to the eventual publication of the *Ethnographic Atlas of Ifugao, a Study of Environment, Culture, and Society in Northern Luzon* (by Harold C. Conklin, with the special assistance of Puggūwon Lupāih and Miklos Pinther; 1980, Yale University Press).

Hal made many trips to Baynīnan over the years, both before and after the *Atlas* was published, indefatigably collecting information about the maintenance and ownership of the pond fields, rituals, harvests, weaving, music, language, pottery, etc. On the occasions when he was able to be away for an entire academic year, the whole family went too. The first family trip was in 1962–63 when our boys were one and three—too young to remember that they participated fully in the activities of the community for twelve months while their father, with the help of their mother and local assistants, was gathering data for the aforementioned opus.

In 1968–69, when Mark and Bruce were seven and nine, we returned to Baynīnan for another full year. The following account, documenting the boys' re-entry into Ifugao culture, was written in 1970 for them to recall better the events that took place during what might otherwise have been their second- and third-grade years in New Haven. Since then, Bruce and Mark have lent their copies of *An Ifugao Notebook* to their friends and recently Bruce enlisted the services of Bethany Taylor who works with him in San Francisco. With great skill and patience she brought a dog-eared and faded typewritten copy of the *Notebook* into the 21st century, making it possible to share the book with readers other than family and friends.

Changes from the original text are minor. Captions have been added to most of the photographs. We decided to keep, rather than change, peoples' names. A glossary of proper names and a few often-used Ifugao words, including a pronunciation guide, can be found at the end of the book. For additional information about our field experiences in Ifugao, see Hal's *Atlas*, referenced above, or go to Mark's website www.markandnoelle.com. You can also reach me at jeanconklin@snet.net.

Jean M. Conklin
New Haven, Connecticut
May 2002

Baynīnan, Banaue, Ifugao

30 September 1968

Up to Ifugao

[The cat]

When I was young my home was a drain under the sidewalk that connects the barbershop and beauty parlor with the main lobby of the Manila Hotel. It was too small for dogs, but large enough for me to run into quickly. From it I had a good view of the backyard and of several dark hallways, and I could see rats and mice on their way to and from the large kitchens. I often went around for free handouts—leftover cheeseburgers or chicken bones—but it was much more sporting to get one's meals on the hoof.

When I had my first family—five very cute orange kittens—I decided to find more pleasant quarters. I moved into a small open courtyard right in the lobby of the hotel. The kittens could play among the potted plants, and while I was off hunting for food, they could take a nap in a gallon-size milk can under the bushes.

Our neighbors were many, including those working in a travel agency, a long distance telephone office, a gift shop, a magazine stand, and a jewelry store. But our very favorite friends were the two pretty girls who operated the Bravo Shop, a small antique store that was crowded with old porcelain dishes, pottery with broken-off handles, faded figurines, and medallions. The two young girls didn't fit in at all with the rest of the furnishings. They had nice smiles, and soldiers on R and R (Rest and Recreation) from Vietnam would stop by to bargain for souvenirs. Whenever the girls made a sale they celebrated by sharing a package of cookies with us.

For a while our special benefactor was an old, stooped-over, white-haired lady. Mrs. Smith had very little to do in her room at the hotel, so one of her amusements was to come down to see us and to bring us a small can of sardines every morning and every afternoon. That, together with the scraps from her meals, tided us over very well. So, except for a very big earthquake (six on the Richter scale; hotel guests were advised that should another tremor occur, "Do not panic. It is not appropriate!"), and the rumor that the manager was planning to rid the hotel of all the cats, life was fairly secure.

When the kittens were about one-and-a-half months old and running about quite freely, two new persons came into our lives. First Bruce, a slender boy of nine years, and several days later his seven-year-old brother, Mark. They spent many hours talking with the Bravo Shop girls, and because they seemed harmless enough, I didn't mind too much when they played with the kittens. Sometimes they did naughty things, like put the kittens high up on a branch, but they always got them down again.

Bruce made his brother promise not to tell their mother about us because she would scold them for playing with stray animals. So when Mark woke up one morning covered with welts, he let his mother think he had come down with some horrible tropical disease and let himself be taken to the doctor. He even managed to keep a straight face and look surprised when the doctor suggested that he had picked up an animal and that what he had were flea bites. He very loyally insisted that he had not picked up any animal. Probably, he said, the fleas lived in the hotel room and had crawled into his bed. He very energetically helped his mother squirt insecticide around the room and his bed.

But Mark was not yet all that good at keeping secrets, and somehow or other he happened to mention the word *cat*. Much to his surprise his mother said, "Well, if they don't belong to anyone maybe we could take them up to Baynīnan with us." Mark didn't wait for the elevator; he *ran* down three flights of stairs to tell Bruce. The boys felt certain that we were strays, but just to make sure they spent the rest of the day checking. The doorman said we were strays. The shopkeepers said no one owned us but perhaps they should ask the manager. The manager said he was going to get rid of all cats, but his secretary said why not ask Mrs. Smith. Mrs. Smith said she would be so happy to know that the cats had a good home. She even gave the boys several cans of sardines and a can opener to take along on the trip.

Of course, all this talking was going on without anyone asking me. When the mother, father, the two boys, and a room boy came around with a couple of baskets, I jumped right through the side of the first basket and we gave them quite a struggle before they managed to get all of us into the second container.

The next twenty-four hours were the worst in my whole life. I could feel the basket being lifted and carried for a short distance. I couldn't see a thing through the wickerwork, but could hear men shouting about footlockers and cartons, about covering everything to keep off the rain, and about not enough strong rope to hold everything down. The kittens went to sleep and I decided it best not to make a sound.

Pretty soon we began to move. I guess we must have been in a truck. The road was so pitted that the truck tipped from side to side and the driver had to stop to tie our basket into place. I was really scared, but since there wasn't a thing I could do, I just gave up and went to sleep. A couple of times the truck stopped, apparently for lunch, then a flat tire, and finally for supper and the night. The next morning they dipped one end of our basket into a basin of water so we could get a drink. Then we were off again. This time the roads were better, but seemed to be winding and climbing (Fig. 1).

Once, very near the end of our trip, we stopped. I could hear a lot of excited voices, directions being given to get a rope, wheels whirling, more shouting, more directions to go to the front and pull forward rather than backward, more wheels whirling. Our truck seemed to be pulling on a great weight that resisted at first, then finally began to follow us. The excited voices calmed down and seemed to be praising my driver, and we were on the way again.

I guess they didn't know about the old Philippine superstition that it is bad luck to have a cat or a monkey as a passenger! They sure took a chance with *six* of us. And from the stories they tell about the other driver, it was a miracle that something more serious than running off the road into a pond field didn't happen—like running off the *other* side of road and plunging straight down hundreds of feet!

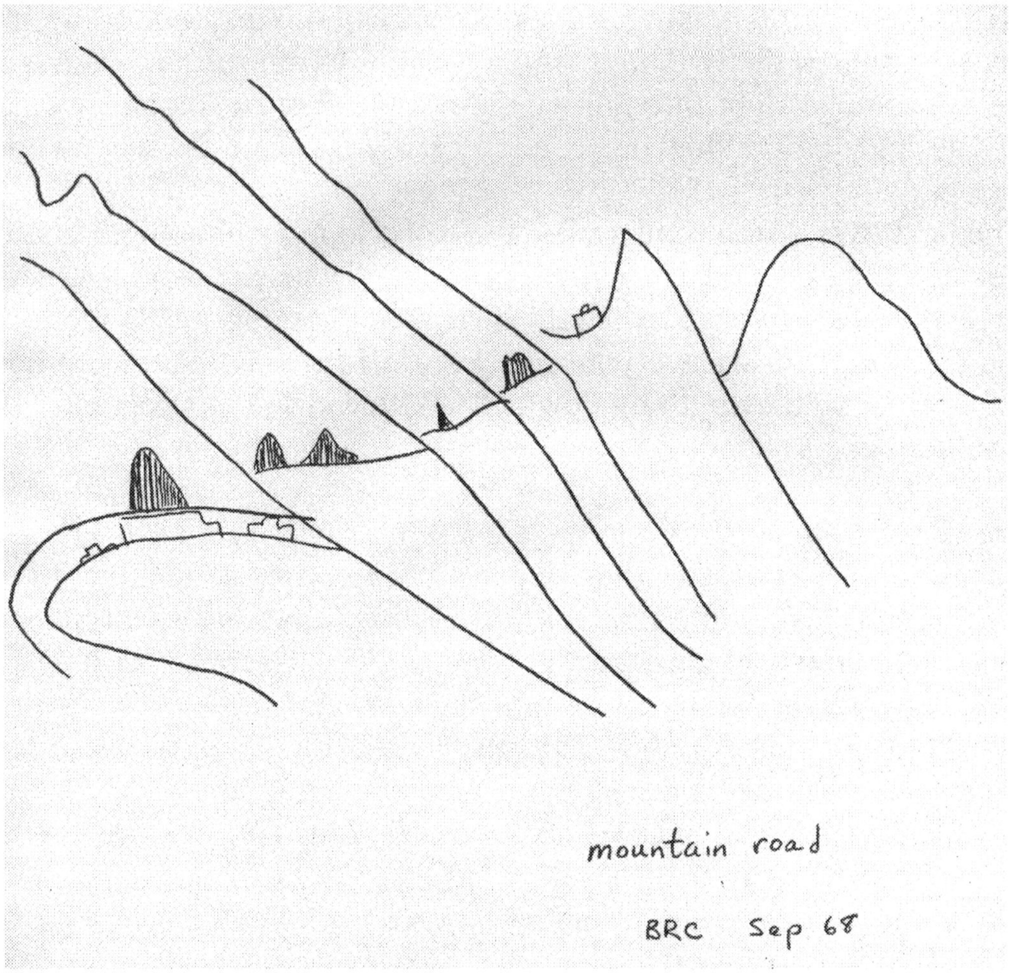

Fig. 1. Bruce's sketch of the road to Banaue.

Well, to get back to my story, just a few minutes more and the ride was over. As the trucks were being unloaded, people were talking and laughing. I couldn't understand what they were saying, but they seemed to be happy to see one another, as if they were old friends who hadn't met for a long time. Someone standing near my basket began giving instructions about us and mentioned that wonderful word "sardines," and before long I could feel the rhythmic movement of being carried on someone's shoulder. And so that is how my new life began.

The kittens and I lived in the Conklin cookhouse. The boys cuddled and played with the babies, and I was so relieved to be safe that I let them pick me up and carry me around too. A beautifully built man with muscles like sweet potatoes came in early every morning and opened a can of sardines for us. We could run out into the houseyard and lie in the sun. The nights were much colder than what we were accustomed to, but the kittens and I curled up in an old cardboard box and were quite comfortable.

The best thing of all were the rats—big healthy ones—scurrying along in the woods, playing under the piles of firewood, stealing into peoples' sleeping huts to nibble on stored foods. Obviously there hadn't been a cat around here for quite a time. I really had a ball. The best hunting time was late afternoon. By six o'clock I usually returned with the first rat. Some nights I got as many as four. One record catch was seven! We couldn't eat that many, but it was great for my ego to listen to everyone boast about me.

After several weeks the kittens were given away. Everyone would have liked to have one, but only very special people were lucky. The first one went to Bu'way, a man of infinite patience who is an unbelievable storehouse of traditional knowledge, a natural linguist, and an excellent teacher. The second one went to Immay, the girl who was Markie's baby-sitter when the family was here six years ago. The third was carried back up the trail to the store on the road, and the fourth was given to the woman, Gonggong, who formerly took care of the family's garden.

A *la''ay* in action.

The fifth wasn't so lucky. It went to a neighbor who has lots of children. It was thought that this would be a good idea since the children could look after the kitten. How wrong they were! The ten-year-old boy kept throwing little #5 onto the roof, laughing and threatening it with a stick when it tried to jump down. But worse than that, the house had a *la''ay*. A *la''ay* (lah'-'eye), whose female counterpart is called an *'ingngi* ('eeng-ngee), is a dangerous creature. These little monsters are unbelievable. They take things from older children or for that matter from everyone. And if for any reason they don't get what they want, they begin screaming and throwing their bodies around on the ground, kicking their legs and beating their fists against the dirt. That shouldn't bother a kitten, but a *la''ay* is usually equipped with a bolo (long bush knife), or at least a pointed stick, and can hit and squeeze. And no one says anything except "Never mind, he doesn't know any better."

Naturally #5 tried to head for our nice safe home at every opportunity. To prevent this, a rope was tied around its neck. I would have thought a rope around the *la''ay*'s neck would have been a better idea. However, everyone to his own taste. Poor #5 was found strangled to death one morning. Bruce and Mark organized a funeral in local style, banged sticks together, and buried #5 in a small cave.

With no immediate family responsibilities I have taken to loafing around for more or less 24 hours at a time—right out in the sun on a good day, or by a cozy fire during a rain. And at night, after the boys have gone into the house to bed, I go to the field lab and curl up right next to the kerosene lamp and stay there until the father goes to bed. He is good company, never says anything, just writes on little pieces of paper, clips them together, and files them away.

Jean and Puggūwon

Right now it is a pretty easy life. After the first 100 or so rats, I have given up hunting except for amusement. Whenever I get hungry I just have to rub up against Puggūwon (poog-GOO-woan), the muscle man who is really softhearted, and he finds something for me to eat. The mother is a soft touch too. They say she doesn't like cats, but I know she likes me. I stand by her place at the table and tap her with my paw. If she doesn't respond properly, I tap her again but with my claws out, and she gives me something from her plate.

I guess I'm pretty lucky that they decided to bring me up here. I think this will be home for a while (Fig. 2).

Fig. 2. Mark's drawing of our house and cookhouse in Baynīnan

13 October 1968

Everything stinks

[Mark]

The kids here are really mean. *Munhamuy di ta''īdan 'amin* (all their feces stink). As soon as I stop crying, I am going to show them. I am going to go out with my slingshot and I am going to shoot them all down. And I am going to yell bad things at them. Especially that little kid, *munhamuy di ta''īna 'ahan* (his especially stinks). He and a bunch of other kids stood around and called out names to me when I had to go down to the outhouse. I tried to throw sticks and stones at them, but they wouldn't stop. I was crying so hard I had to stay down there until finally Mommy came around to find out where I was.

Daddy tried to tell me that kids are mean all over the world, but that didn't help me any. Mommy told him she didn't blame me for getting mad, so Daddy said, "OK, I will teach you what to say." And what he taught me was really cool, man. I can hardly wait until somebody tries something funny again. And I know a lot of naughty poses and gestures to make too, and no one had to teach me those.

Brucie and I are trying hard to make friends, but so far we have nothing much to show for our efforts. There are lots of kids around, every size, and mostly smaller than us. *Munhamuy di pūhugdan 'amin* (all their belly buttons stink). Some of them have gone to school and know a little English, but they still can't understand us and we can't understand them either. Sometimes I think they will understand us if we act out stuff, then maybe they will think we are funny, and then they will like us. So me and Brucie pretend wrestling or judo, or silly things like rock and roll or sword fighting. But usually something goes wrong, and somebody gets hurt and begins to cry. Sometimes it's me, sometimes it's Brucie, and sometimes it's someone else. And I'm not sorry because *munhamuy di butlīdan 'amin* (everyone's you-know-what stinks).

Mark playing cards with his small friend.

Another thing that makes me mad is when I try to imitate what they say and I say it wrong, they just laugh and it makes me feel stupid. Well, I'm going to knock them silly. Anyway *munhamuy di pūlongda* (their anuses stink). It sure is a good thing that Daddy taught me these things. It makes me feel better already.

There are three little kids who often play near our place. Their names are Ālen, Pēlek, and Nehtol. They have little knives and they chop things and make stuff out of sticks. They say words over and over to me, and they seem friendly, but pretty soon they go someplace else and I am left all by myself again.

There is one kid who doesn't say mean things or go away—because she can't talk yet and she can't walk either. I like to go over to visit her. We talk baby talk and I do funny things to make her laugh, and right now she is the only real friend I have. One day her mother tied her onto my back with a blanket sling and let me carry her.

Every once in a while things don't seem too bad, like when I went up to Līwang with Bangluy (pyahng-loy) to see a carabao get killed. Bangluy is friendly and strong and he wouldn't let anything happen to me or Brucie. Here is a picture of Līwang and what the carabao (water buffalo) looked like after it was killed (Fig. 3).

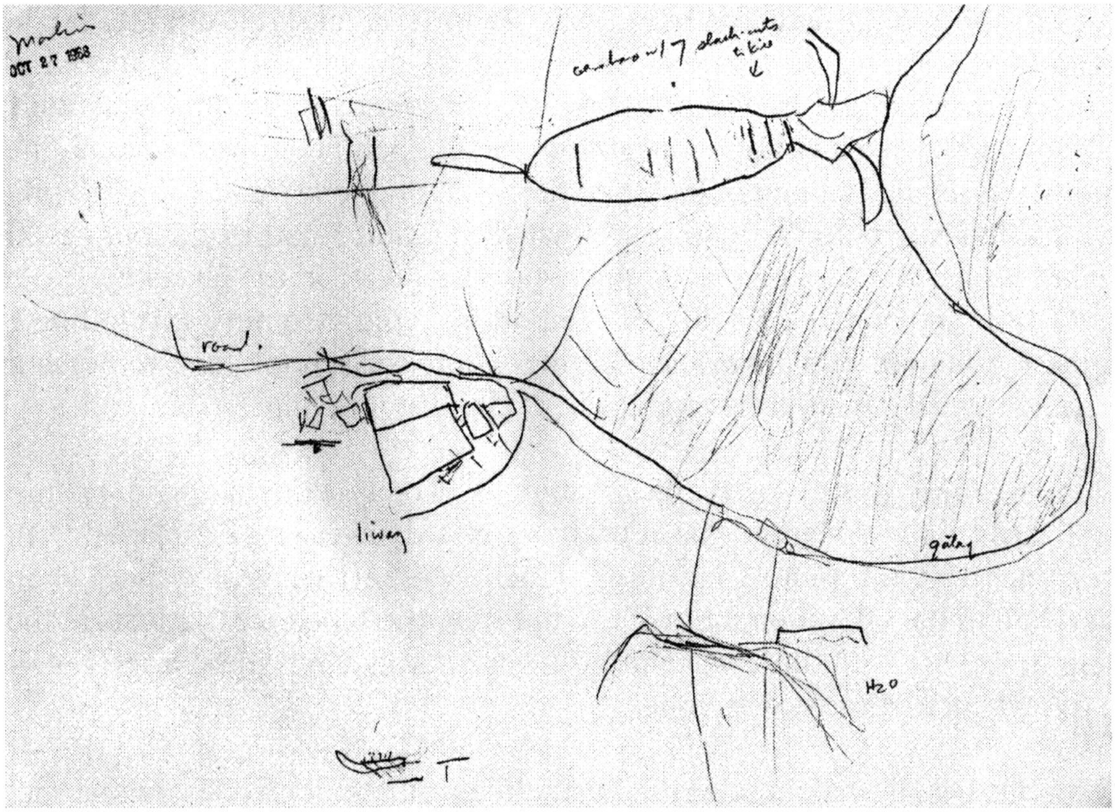

Fig. 3. Mark's sketch of the carabao at Līwang. Mark represented our family because the rest of us couldn't make it. He brought home a meat share.

30 October 1968

A neat place with lots of animals

[Bruce]

Just one second. OK, OK, just one second! Why do they always have to call me when I am in the middle of something interesting. One day I was saving a baby chick. You see, mother hens walk around clucking, and stop often to scratch up the dirt to hunt for bugs. All the little chicks run along after her, chirping, and learning how to scratch the dirt. If the chicks get scattered, the mother hen runs around in circles clucking, and rounds them up again. Well, I was following these chicks and one stupid one got behind a post. He could hear his mother clucking but he couldn't see her. He got excited and began flapping his wings, but he couldn't figure out what to do, and I had to go and get him and take him to the rest of the family who had gone pretty far away by that time. Right in the middle of doing this important thing, Mommy was telling me that recess was over. It's always something—time for school, time to brush my teeth, time to take a bath, time to go to bed. OK, I'm coming.

This is a neat place. All kinds of animals. Today Puggūwon found me a flying lizard (Fig. 4). Man, it was cool. It really did have wings. I played with it all morning, then put it into a jar during lunch. Mommy suggested that I should let it go late in the afternoon, but when I put it on the fence post, it just sat there looking at me as if it didn't want to go away. It was even there after I took a bath, but by suppertime it was gone.

The man who was in charge of making our schoolroom made me a slingshot. I love to walk around in the woods below our place looking for birds and insects, and if I am lucky, maybe someday I'll find a snake. I always carry my Swiss Army knife. Daddy put it on the end of a cord so I can sling it around my neck and shoulder and not have to take it off when I use it. It is fun to whittle on sticks and make things out of bamboo.

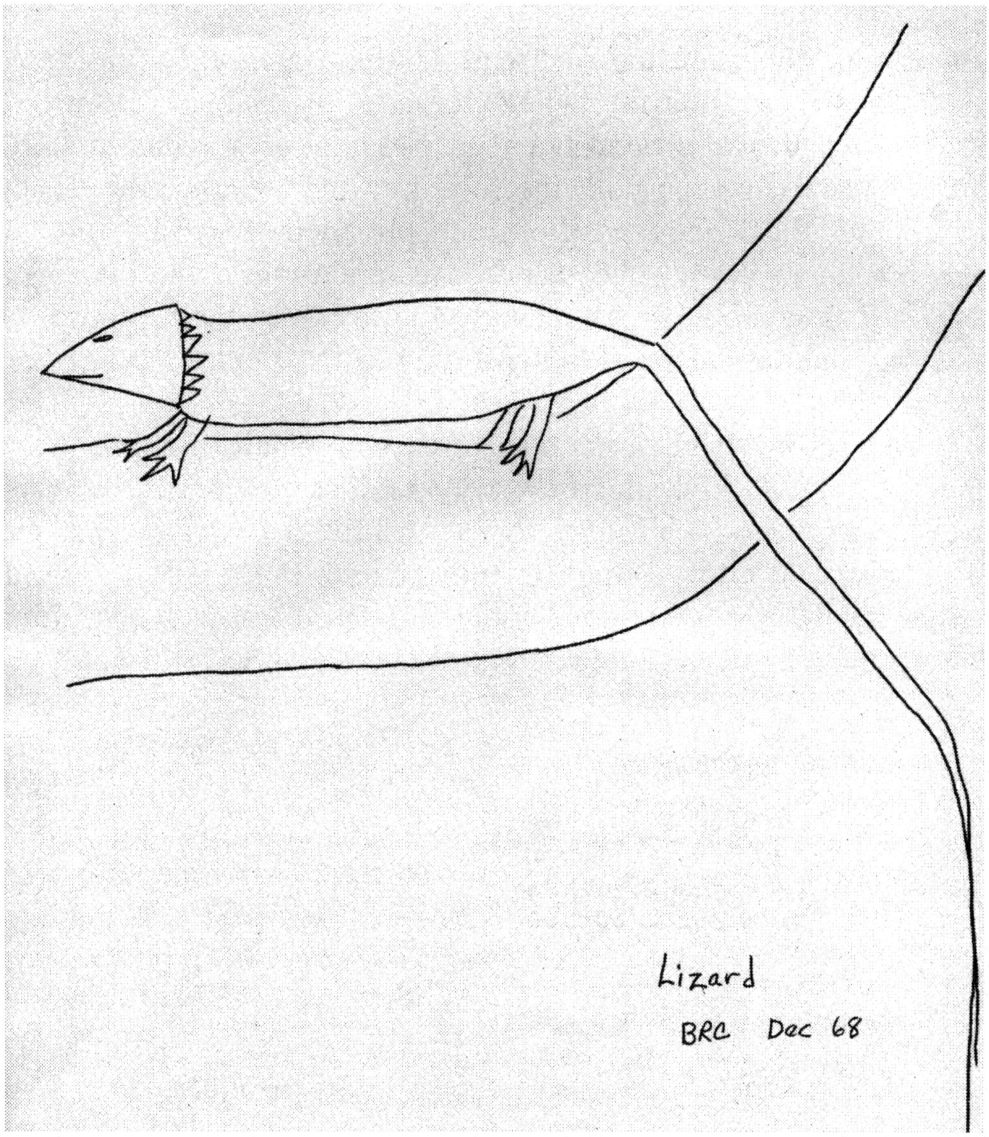

Fig. 4. Bruce's flying lizard.

Living here is like living on a farm. We can look out our school window and see dragonflies, butterflies, birds, and funny things like one little pig trying to put his sperm into another little pig. One little pig even tried to put it into his MOTHER, but he couldn't make it. Me and Mark were laughing and laughing, and Mommy told us he was just practicing and to go back to reading.

All of us love to watch the pigs eat. There is a mother with seven little piglets next door. Every morning when Gotya (kot-yah) begins to prepare their breakfast, the pigs crowd around her legs. Sometimes she has to stop and hit them with a stick so she can pour the food into the trough. They all push and shove each other for a good position, and put their feet right into the food. When they are finished, their faces and heads are a mess, and the food is even splattered over their bodies. Whenever Mommy sees them, she always has something to say about the way I look after a meal.

The animals are cool, but I have to agree with Mark, the kids around here aren't the greatest. I think the best way is just to go off by myself. Or sometimes just together with Mark. There is a little stream that runs down near our place, and we like to go there to build dams. Pretty soon the kids come around to see what we are doing, and before you know it, we are playing together even though we can't understand what each other is saying.

One thing the boys here do that is lots of fun is to wade around in the *payo* (pond field) hunting for fish and snails. It is all right to do this now because the new rice hasn't been planted yet. The water isn't very deep but you sink down into the soft mud and sometimes the mud is way up to your shorts. The boys catch *dolog* (mudfish) and *yūyu* (a Japanese fish, they say) and they give us some to take home to eat. The fish is bony, but it is fun to eat something that you helped to catch. "Japanese fish" swimming among the "Chinese cabbage." That's funny!

You can do all this without knowing much Ifugao, and there are some times when it is very helpful *not* to know the language. Like when a bunch of us take off all our clothes and wallow in one of the *payo*. The sun makes the shallow water warm, and we get covered with the dark mud while we are fooling around and splashing each other and chasing ducks and screaming. Pretty soon we can hear the mothers shouting at us to get out. But Markie and me pretend we don't understand, and since we don't get out, the other kids don't get out either. Finally Mommy shouts to us in English and we have to get out. She says she doesn't mind, but that the people are afraid that we will get itchy from the pond-field water because of the ducks, or something.

Well, like I said before, this is a fun place. And if I am lucky, maybe someday I'll find a snake.

30 November 1968

The truth

[Jean]

The title of this chapter is a private joke requiring an explanation. Several years ago Hal and I were having dinner with another couple who had just returned from a field trip. The conversation turned quickly to a comparison of field experiences and a friendly competition as to whose group was more exotic.

"Ours is almost self-sufficient; they still weave homespun-cotton blankets and skirts."

"So what. If they don't drink anything alcoholic, how could they be interesting?"

"The gong rhythms are so intricate that a musicologist tried all day and couldn't figure them out."

"If he had had some of our rice beer on hand he could have done it."

As the exchange became more exaggerated, the other wife began to modify her husband's statements with, "Well, that's not exactly the way it is," or "Oh, it isn't really all that good." Finally the husband good-naturedly suggested that they had better write two separate ethnographies, to which she replied, "I don't write ethnographies, I write the truth."

The truth is that field work isn't all fun and games. The minor details of getting settled don't always seem so minor. For example, our one-room house is converted into a one-room bedroom by rolling out the woven mats. It took about a week of experimenting to find the best combination of blankets to use under and over us. It was a whole month before I thought of putting safety pins at the bottom edges of blankets and sheets so that I can determine the head end from the foot end even without a light. It seems more hygienic to keep the same end of the sheet reserved for our heads because at bedtime our faces

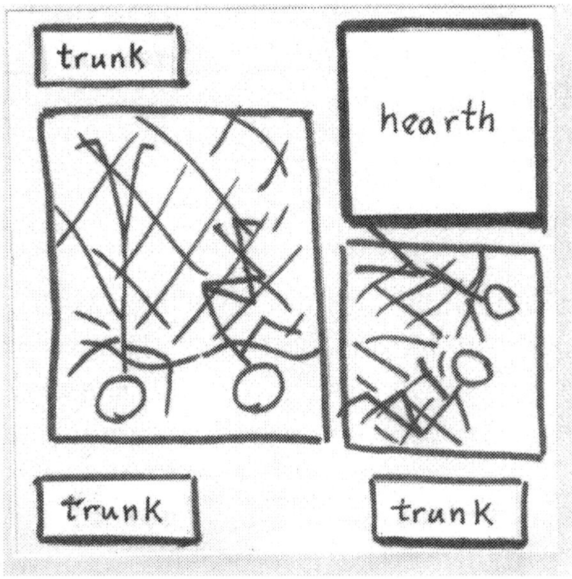

might be clean but our feet never are. Two pins tells me it is the extra long blanket for Hal; and two pins on Mark's sheet means it is the dirtiest and is next in line to be washed. Finally I thought of bringing a basin and kettle of water into the house so that the boys could rinse some of the mud from their feet before going to bed.

It also took a while to work out the best timing for bathing the boys. Known factors are an unroofed bathing enclosure, late afternoon downpours, boys dirty enough to need soap and water, and no real daylight after 5 or 5:30. It is tricky to get them in from playing as late as possible so that they have the minimum amount of time to go back out to get dirty again; but not too late so that there is enough light to look for new insect bites and infections while I'm washing them. They hate to stop playing, but they soon learned that the longer they wait after I call, the cooler the kettle of water gets; and the last one to respond is less sure that there will be half a kettle of hot water left for him.

I even had trouble working out my own bathing problems. At first I thought I'd do what I usually do at home—clean up before going to bed. However, nights are cool, breezy, and more than a couple of times, my "bath" got rained out. And one time each I, (a) forgot to ask for the cookhouse key and couldn't heat the water, (b) had the key but found the burners needed kerosene, and (c)

discovered the water containers empty. On the occasions when all conditions were "go," I found that, while I was busy swatting the mosquitoes, little frogs jumped up my legs. And illumination from the flashlight, though enough to attract all insects within half a kilometer, was not sufficient to show up the caterpillars and spiders that were crawling on the towel and into my clothing. I soon switched to the middle of the day for bathing.

I have the feeling that everyone is watching me, not maliciously probably, just out of curiosity maybe. Now that I am adjusted, or as adjusted as I'm going to get, I can even go down to the outhouse with all the little kids standing around shouting, "Jean is going down to the outhouse" and it hardly annoys me at all.

The funniest thing about the outhouse is that they keep improving the way to get to it. Someone no doubt has reported my slipping and sliding. At first they cut notches into the slope; then they put slabs of tough tree-fern stems down so the steps wouldn't get muddy or slippery; recently they widened the pathway. Finally they used some leftover rocks to make a flagstone walk from our place to the steps. But the outhouse is the same old outhouse that we had six years ago, unless one wants to argue that since all of the original material has been replaced, it is no longer the same outhouse. I say it is the same hole, so it is the same outhouse. Old or new, it is unique. We enter and squat over a deep pit. The pigs enter a cave at the bottom of the pit and clean up. A great invention, but nevertheless, I always try to arrange to finish all essential business before 5 p.m. After that I worry that I won't see the spiders, or might step on a loose board, or drop into the hole if the kids have forgotten to put the lid back on. I better remind Puggūwon to replace the floor boards. Hal says that at the rate we are now going, we are only two steps away from the reinvention of the flush toilet.

We try to keep up a six-mornings-a-week school schedule so that a day missed now and then for a local event doesn't put the boys too far behind. I hope to cover the essential portions of second and third grade work during these half-day sessions, leaving the rest of the day free for them to enjoy being here and for me to help with the field materials.

Lessons in progress.

Local events are pretty hard to miss. During October and especially November, the small children in many of the local families were having runny noses and coughs, and it was felt that perhaps the bones of an esteemed old aunt were in need of a little attention and a new blanket. About a week ago they brought out her bone bundle, sacrificed a large pig on the first day, a carabao on the next, and another pig on the third day. On "pig" days Bruce and Mark sat on their benches trying to read, but were really straining their ears to catch the first ear-shattering squeal. Then they shot out of the door in time for the kill and for the burning and scraping off of the hair, a messy job that is well-suited for small boys.

On carabao day I simply declared an official school holiday. The poor unsuspecting animal was brought into the hamlet, and all of the boys led it around and took turns riding on its back. Relatives gathered from near and far, and finally several prominent male members of the community did away with the beast with a few well-placed bolo chops.

The meat distribution scene that followed was typically Ifugao. Here is what happens. Every kin group plans to take home as large a meat share as it can get away with. When the actual butchering takes place and distribution begins, every group but one thinks that the choice shares are going to the wrong persons. The more aggressive kinsmen don't wait to be called; they come forward to stake their claims. Everyone is waving his bolo, and everyone is shouting. Often someone grabs a large share and makes a run for it, usually succeeding in spite of the women and children who try to catch him.

After everything edible was given away, the rest of the animal was cleaned up in a big hurry and dumped into boiling water. Lunch was served as quickly as possible before tempers had a chance to flare up again. It was well past noon and people were hungry. Besides that, visitors who had traveled some distance were anxious to leave in order to reach home before dark, and the local hosts were anxious to have them leave in order to have a little peace and quiet again.

Boys playing with the carabao in front of our house.

As it turned out this time, peace and quiet were still a few hours away. The little girl who got the carabao urinary bladder (inflated and tied, it's like a big balloon) and was playing ball with it, was chased by a little boy who didn't get the urinary bladder and who was carrying a long pointed iron spike. The man who paid for the carabao yelled at the head priest and accused him of an unfair distribution. All the kids were bickering and fighting because they were overtired.

But now, no one has a cold or runny nose, so I guess the old aunt is cozy and warm in her new blanket and the ritual was a success.

What I need now is an improvement in our own food situation. The few canned goods that I purchased in Manila are gone. Hal discouraged me from bringing up a large supply but was more than cooperative about eating his share. It hurts me when the kids say at the end of a meal, "Are we having anything else to eat?"

Puggūwon was originally hired to take care of our house structures and to do the cooking. One day I found sketches of "cowboys" that he had made on the backs of canned good labels. Hal immediately encouraged him to use our typing paper to make sketches of things going on in the community. He took on this assignment with great enthusiasm and was soon producing detailed diagrams and sketches of terrace building, rituals, and house construction. Three times a day he interrupted his drawing to prepare our meals.

Although sweet potatoes are considered a poor man's substitute for rice, we suggested having them for breakfast. So for almost a week, we had sweet potatoes and either maple syrup or honey—until both bottles were empty. Then we opened our one jar of peanut butter and found that sweet potatoes and peanut butter were not so bad; and we have been able to continue this combination because tiny, unhomogenized, dust-covered jars of peanut butter are available in Banaue. I find the contents a little too rancid, so I alternate between sweet potatoes and rancid peanut butter, and sweet potatoes and local brown sugar.

Lunch and supper menus are determined by what is available—rice and canned meat, occasionally rice and ritual meat, rice and cooked sweet potato leaves, rice and cooked cabbage, rice and canned fruit, rice and soy sauce, rice and cooked onions, rice and catsup, rice and cooked mudfish from the fields, rice and beans, rice and snails. The low point was the day we had rice and noodles.

Desserts are pretty limited now that we have finished off the box of candy bars and several tins of cookies. Banaue has a bakery whose cookies are large and rubbery when fresh, and hard as rocks if old. Their rolls aren't bad. In fact, they seemed quite good until someone told me that the baker has an incurable skin disease.

There is an unused plot down near the map room. We could ask Gonggong to start another garden for us like she did the last time we were here. We could try, again, to spread the word that we are anxious to buy surplus vegetables that otherwise would be taken to market. We could order canned goods—and even fresh vegetables—from Baguio, but I was really hoping that we could work out a local solution to maintain a minimum level of nutrition and still remain inconspicuous. Eggs and chickens are usually available in Banaue but it is said that the chickens in the region have contracted some kind of sickness, and those that aren't dying have stopped laying eggs. However, even without the sickness, I would be opposed to purchasing local eggs and poultry for everyday use because these items are considered luxuries and are reserved for ritual events by our neighbors.

I'm going to have to make a firm decision soon. Meanwhile I am stuffed with sweet potatoes, rice, and Banaue cookies—gaining weight, but feeling hungry.

15 December 1968

Their problems are my problems

[Hal]

Here I am—no telephone, no committee meetings, no annual reports—free to concentrate on my own work! It's a near perfect field situation. Only minor repairs were needed on the living and working quarters that we set up in 1962–63. Plans for checking and adding to all phases of the research have been made with the full cooperation of our neighbors, and everyone seems happy to have us back.

No matter how hard one tries to settle in quietly, there is no doubt that an anthropologist disrupts the normal comings and goings of a community. A great deal of diplomacy goes into keeping the big brass happy at the same time that one is singling out persons with special skills without regard to their position in the local social system. Perhaps the most extreme example of this was our choice last time of Immay as Markie's baby-sitter. Overnight she became a member of a high prestige family. She and, fortunately for us, all those who were helping us, had the great good sense to play down the special privilege aspects of their newly found work.

Ottēngan, the traditional ritual head of the community, remains in charge. We keep him informed of all plans, he often makes suggestions, and nothing is carried out without his final approval. Most importantly he has full responsibility for our ritual obligations and needs.

Puggūwon has taken to cartography with a passion. His work is meticulous and beautiful. And he continues to take care of our house, water supply, and meals as well. Būgan (POO-kyahn), qualified to be an elementary school teacher, has joined forces with Bu'way on the linguistic and census materials. Together they will work with Ottēngan on the pond-field chains of title.

I feel well in control of the situation, even feel comfortable with the language. As I said before, it's a *near* perfect setup. The three people who give me the most severe attacks of anxiety are Jean, Bruce, and Mark. I really thought that the kids would have made their adjustments long ago. I thought kids learned new languages quickly. Instead they are constantly scrapping with the local kids and with each other. And from the way Jean screams at them during the morning school sessions, I gather that they are giving her a hard time too.

Jean's complaining bothers me the most. It is hard to give full attention to working when she is griping about the food, the weather, the bugs, the kids, and everyone. I asked her if she wanted to go back to the States. She said she'd stay but that didn't mean that she had to like it.

Occasionally it seems as though things are getting better. Then something comes along to set everything back again. Like yesterday's visit to Kinnākin. I assured them that it was an easy hike; the local kids use the trail to go to school each day. Mark thought he was going to die of thirst. And Jean had a terrible time. She seemed unhappy on even the gentlest of slopes. Good thing she really doesn't have to do a lot of walking. There is plenty of deskwork that she can help out with. That reminds me, I want to reorganize the files. If she can help me do that, I'll be able to find any slip in seconds. Better get to that as soon as possible. Maybe I'll work all night.

January 1969

Mark

[Jean]

Five months. Seems like fifteen. Mark can hold his own in most everyday situations, and can effectively tease playmates when he gets a mind to. He says a lot, and adds gestures when the going gets rough. He usually understands what people are telling him, and is also willing to use his intuition. "I didn't know what he was saying, but I think he was telling me to stop, so I did." When he isn't just plain playing, he likes to help—feed the pigs in the morning, put the chickens back into their cages in the afternoon, and chop firewood. Occasionally he leaves his bolo in a careless way and has to suffer the punishment of not being able to use it for a week.

Mark and Kalluh.

He is playing the role of a "roving big brother." He goes next door to play with the baby for a while. Then he wanders to the next house and helps the boy pound and winnow rice. Then he notices that a friend's older brother is teasing him, so he goes over and scares the hell out of the big brother. All he has to do is stand near somebody and make threatening motions. His very size is enough to scare anyone.

Probably Mark's outstanding moment so far was the time he got drunk. Hal was up in the house entertaining a visitor. Mark joined them and began tasting the *bayah* (rice beer). Hal cautioned him not to take too much and then went back to talking. Very shortly Mark started down the ladder, lost his footing about halfway down and fell backwards to the ground, pulled himself up, and began reeling around on the house terrace. He shouted, "I am drunk," in Ifugao, and "I want to dance," in English, over and over again. At first I thought he was imitating Ifugao drunken behavior and was admiring how well he was doing, but soon saw from the glazed look in his eyes that he wasn't kidding. For half an hour he staggered and shouted, and had to be supported and restrained in order to keep him from hurting himself. In the cookhouse he tried several times to knock the dishes off the table and once managed to lift one end of the table in an attempt to dump everything. Finally he got sick and after much coaxing he agreed to climb into the house to rest. He retched and heaved for another hour or so, and said he never wanted to get drunk again.

Mark's Ifugao world is this hamlet. He knows it and its residents well. In response to an assignment to draw a map of a place you know, he produced the sketch on the next page (Fig. 5). The only error of omission is a house occupied only occasionally by a woman who has no children. In the security of our cookhouse he can give a side-splitting, half-hour performance pantomiming the betel exchange, Ifugao nose-blowing, rituals, and key Baynīnan neighbors.

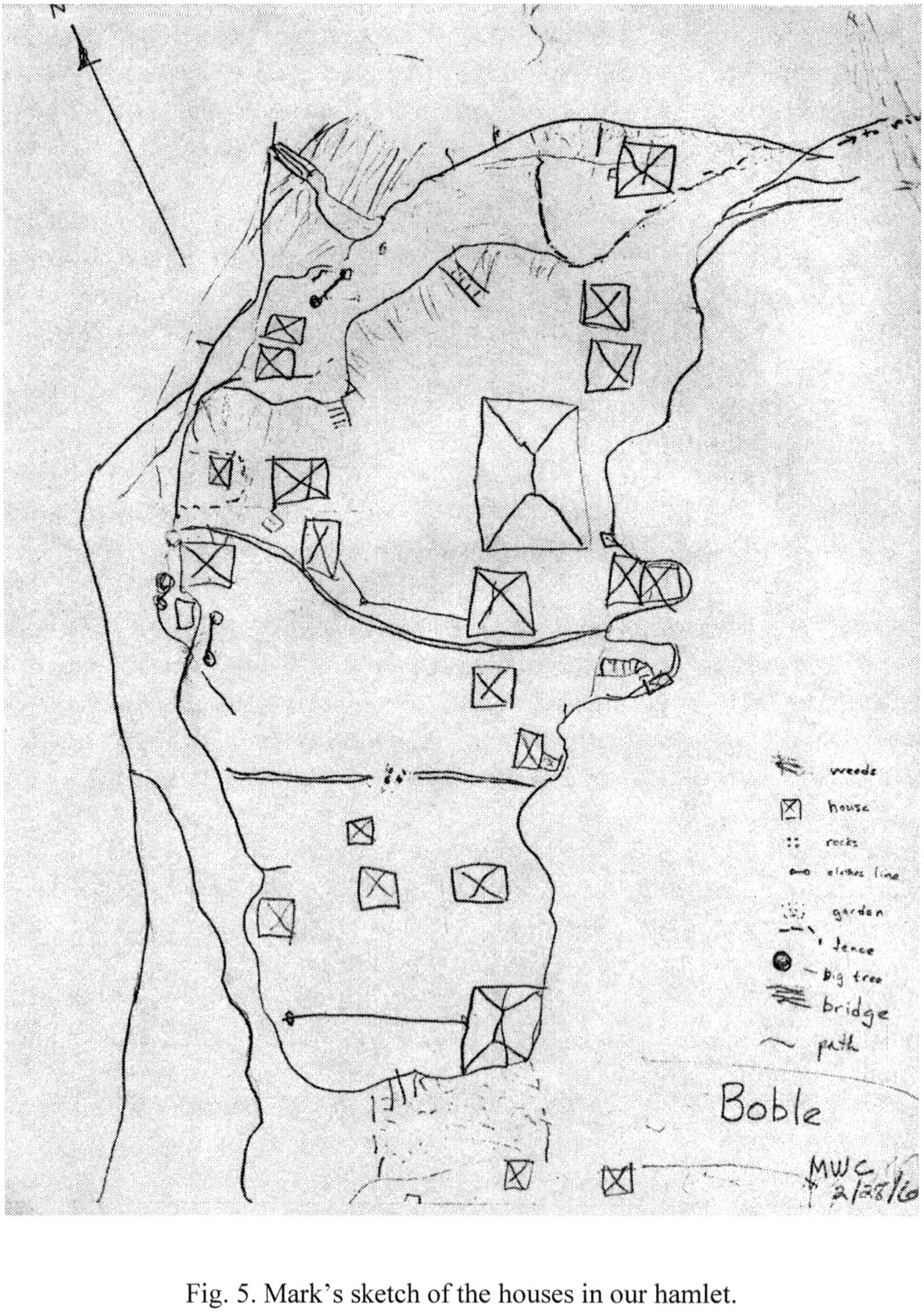

Fig. 5. Mark's sketch of the houses in our hamlet.

Bruce

[Jean]

In response to the same mapmaking assignment, Bruce drew one (Fig. 6) that included our hamlet, neighboring house clusters, and the surrounding woods. He has noted steep and rocky places, dried-up fields, and streams. Pugguwon, our official mapmaker, attests that the paths and shortcuts as drawn are true to a turn. Bruce is rarely separated from his slingshot; in fact he sleeps with it around his neck, and using green coffee beans for ammunition he combs the woods for anything that moves. He is the one who usually locates and brings up the firewood, and, after all that work, is generous enough to allow Mark to chop up half of it.

We bought a monkey (it seemed like a good idea when I suggested getting one) that is officially known as Bruce's, and he has taken on the responsibility of looking after it. This includes not only feeding it, but also protecting it from the local population who delight in offering it things it can't eat, or offering things it can eat only to withdraw the food at the last moment. This form of teasing is hard enough to take, but when someone throws sticks and stones, Bruce is out there fighting. As a reward, the monkey recognizes his protector and eats out of Bruce's hand though he will swing out and try to scratch and bite others. Sometimes it seems that Bruce prefers the monkey's company to tangling with the local kids. I sympathize with him. In most cases I think I would make the same choice.

Kallat (rubber bands) are the rage just now, and Bruce has taken on the competition with a vengeance. At first he and Mark worked out a kind of insurance plan. They shared each other's winnings to cover themselves when they lost. But Mark either lost or gave away so many rubber bands that Bruce decided to go it alone.

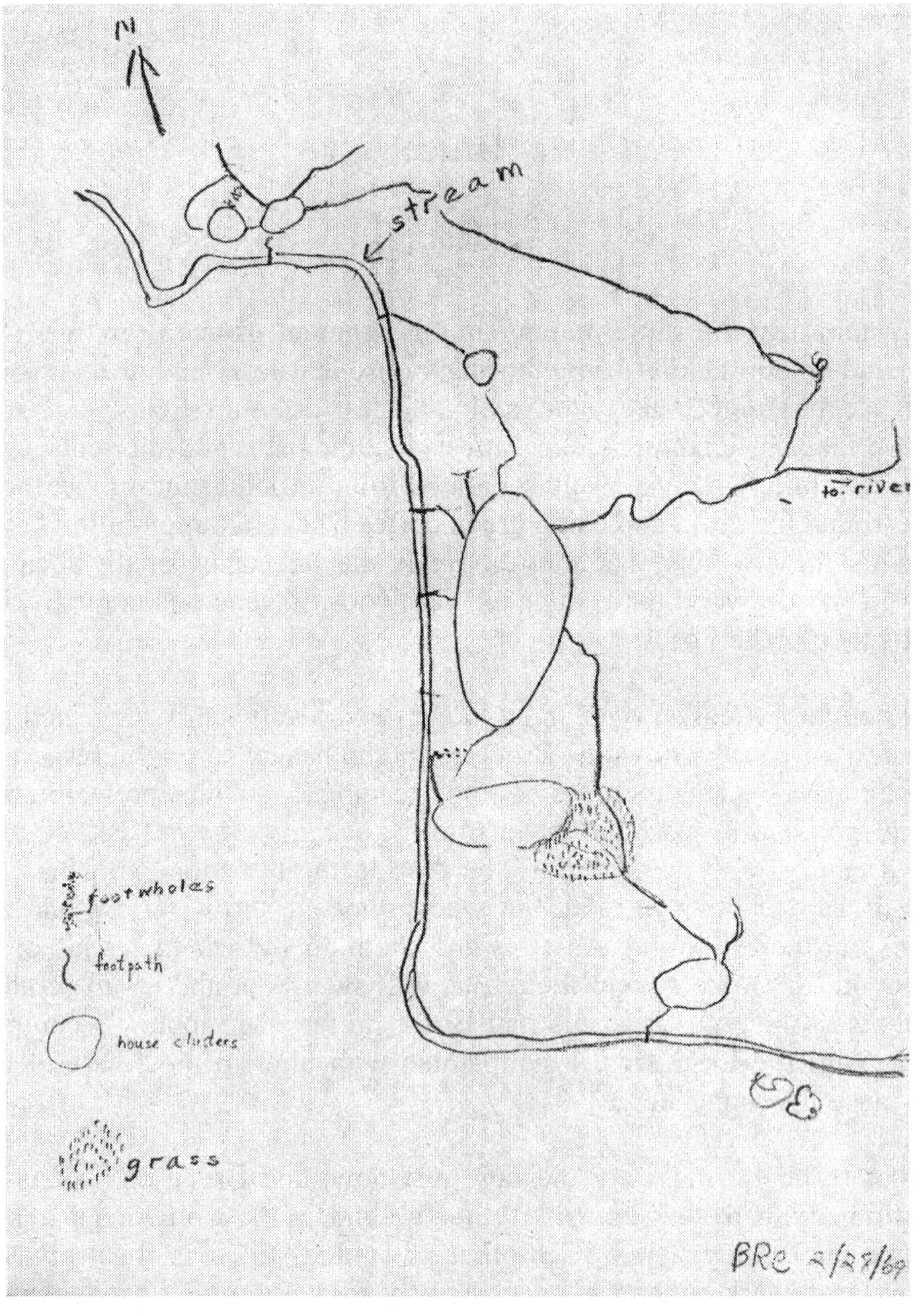

Fig. 6. Bruce's map of our hamlet, neighboring house clusters, and surrounding woods.

The game usually involves two players, each with his/her own rubber bands, and requires only the smooth exterior wall of an Ifugao house and some clear ground space. Before starting the game, the players decide how many *kallat* will be a "set"—three, or five, or whatever.

The first player places a *kallat* on the palm of his/her hand and throws it against the wall allowing it to fall on the ground. The second player does the same but tries to make his/her *kallat* fall as close as possible to the first player's *kallat*. The players continue taking turns until the "set" is completed. The winner, who takes all, is the player whose *kallat* touches one of the opponent's *kallat*; or whose *kallat* came the closest to touching one of the opponent's *kallat*. The rules seem flexible and in fact often seem to be invented on the spot, but the general aim of the game is to win as many rubber bands as possible. One's entire collection is carried around all day, either on one's wrist or looped together in long, long chains and worn around the neck.

Bruce started out with one rubber band that he found on the ground (the American ones of which we have hundreds are no good; it has to be a local round kind that comes with one-centavo candies). Slowly he has built up his collection to about 70! He spends part of each day sorting these out—by color, or by how well they bounce, or by tens. Then he goes out to find someone to play with.

His devious methods win more *kallat* than friends. When he finds himself running low, he challenges little kids so he can beat them. Or when he finds himself pitted against an expert, he often suggests that they play against our house. Our house is higher than many of the houses, and Bruce is taller than most of the players, so the good short player usually loses to the poor tall player.

For the first couple of months Bruce was behind Mark language-wise, but there's no difference now. He's right in there with everyone else, and having a great time.

17 January 1969

A vengeance rite

[Bruce]

Well, my Swiss Army knife is gone. Someone must be very happy. It wasn't exactly my fault. This morning I went with Puggūwon, Bu'way and Āma (we call our father *Āma* now and our mother *Īna*, which just means 'father' and 'mother'), to watch the burial ritual for a murdered man. Markie and Īna didn't go because the trails would have been too slippery. Īna said, "You better leave your knife here."

But Āma said, "It's OK, take it, you might need it."

Group of male relatives arriving from a distant settlement.

We hiked way up to the edge of Baynīnan and into Līwang. Whenever we stopped to look around Āma took pictures and once he borrowed my knife to fix a screw. Then he gave it back but I guess I forgot to put it around my neck again. Anyway when Puggūwon and Bu'way went back to look for it, it was already gone.

Except for that, it was a beautiful day and I saw lots of interesting things. The man was murdered four days ago. They say he was a very quiet person who worked hard all the time. He was making a new field and in fact that is probably the reason he is dead now. The other day he started out to work, but someone told him that Ottēngan had declared a ritual holiday. He turned back and was working in his houseyard when someone came around, shot him, and slashed him to death. Everyone thinks it was the person with whom he had been in disagreement over land and water rights. But no one is talking and the official police records in Banaue will list the incident as unsolved.

When someone is killed, the funeral and burial rites are different from those for a person who just dies. For a murdered person all the male relatives come together to assure the dead man that his murder will not go unavenged. They come in groups from all the neighboring settlements, walking along the trails and edges of the terraces, rhythmically banging on their shields or special wooden clappers, letting the people in general and the murderer in particular know that they are on the way to the vengeance ritual.

Today there were about 200 men dancing their way to the burial site from four different directions. They looked very strong and ready to fight with their loincloths swinging, no shirts to hide their muscles, sheathed bolos hanging from their sides, and wide white palm-spathe headbands with long narrow blood-red leaves sticking out.

It took a long time for all of them to reach the ceremonial site, but finally we went up to where the man's house was (Fig. 7). I wondered then how his children could play there, it was so steep all around. The man was propped up against one of his house posts, the head that was almost cut off was tied to his body, and he had a spear secured in each hand. You could see the place where the bullet went in and all the cuts all over his shoulders and arms, and his body was all swollen and smelly. An older woman was sitting near him, poking at him with a weaver's sword, and shouting at his spirit not to go to sleep but to come back and bother the murderer.

Avenging kinsmen dancing their way to the ritual.

Meanwhile, the dancers went to the top of a ridge and got into a big circle to decide which man would be the one directly responsible for revenge. Someone in the center cuts off a chicken's head. The chicken's body runs around and whoever it falls down near is supposed to be the one to kill one of the murderer's male relatives. This time the chicken ran out of the circle and didn't end up near anyone, so it meant no one person would be responsible.

Then they went to see what kind of animal was caught in the woven-bamboo trap. The type of animal would tell something about how and when the revenge would take place. This turned out to be a failure too since nothing was caught.

Finally they wrapped the body up and carried it away. And we all went home too.

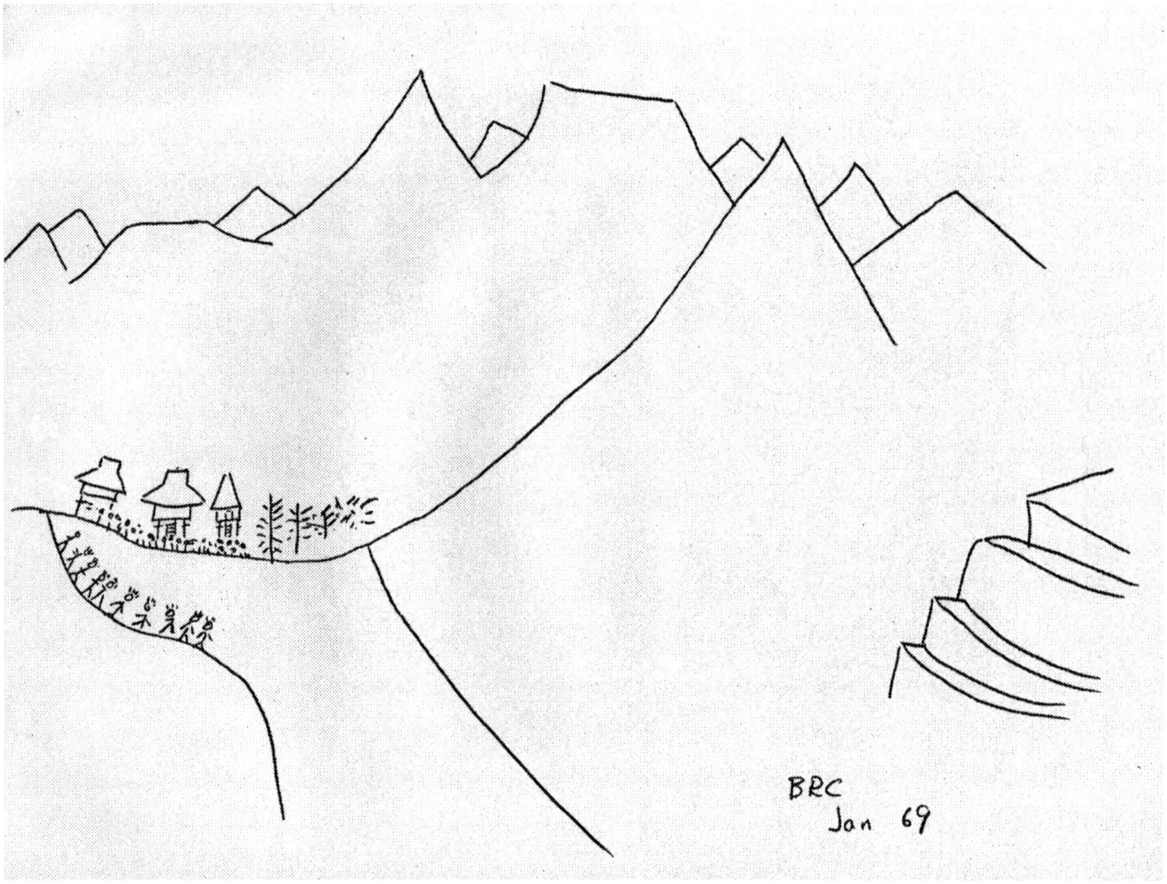

Fig. 7. Funeral dancers approaching murder victim's house cluster.

11 March 1969

The end of a fighter

[The fighting cock]

I'll have to tell my story quickly. In a few minutes I'm going to be served for lunch. It doesn't seem to me to be a very fair thing to happen as a result of doing such a normal natural thing—just crowing when I woke up. The trouble seems to be that it wasn't dawn when I woke up, it was only ten or eleven at night! Maybe where you are it is all right to crow whenever you want to, but around here it's considered to be a bad omen to crow at the wrong time. No one can say for sure of what it is a bad sign, but just for good measure the custom is to get rid of the omen—me. Oh, oh, here they come now.

"Puggūwon, what are you going to do with that rooster?"

"You're going to have it for lunch."

"Oh, no, you can't do that. Choose another. He is one of our best fighters. He can even beat Kalluh's rooster."

"That's too bad; but he crowed last night and that is supposed to be very bad luck. Maybe someday you will find another good fighting cock."

"Not as good as this one. Oh well. Puggūwon, let me help you. I know how to do it. I'll hold the legs and wings. You hold the beak and cut the throat. Do you have something to catch the blood in?"

5 April 1969

Snake!

[Mark]

Today Bruce, Pēlek, Yūbel, and I went way over to where Kohemmay was weeding her field. We were helping to burn the weeds when we heard Ekka shouting, "Snake! Snake!"

We ran over right away and started throwing stones and rocks at it. Someone hit it, but its tongue was still wiggling. Yūbel had a knife and he went over and slashed at it a couple of times, but it was still alive. The kids got more stones, and I shouted to Bruce, "Hit it some more."

Bruce banged it with a big rock until it was pushed into the ground. Here is a picture Brucie drew of Kohemmay carrying Ekka away from the snake.

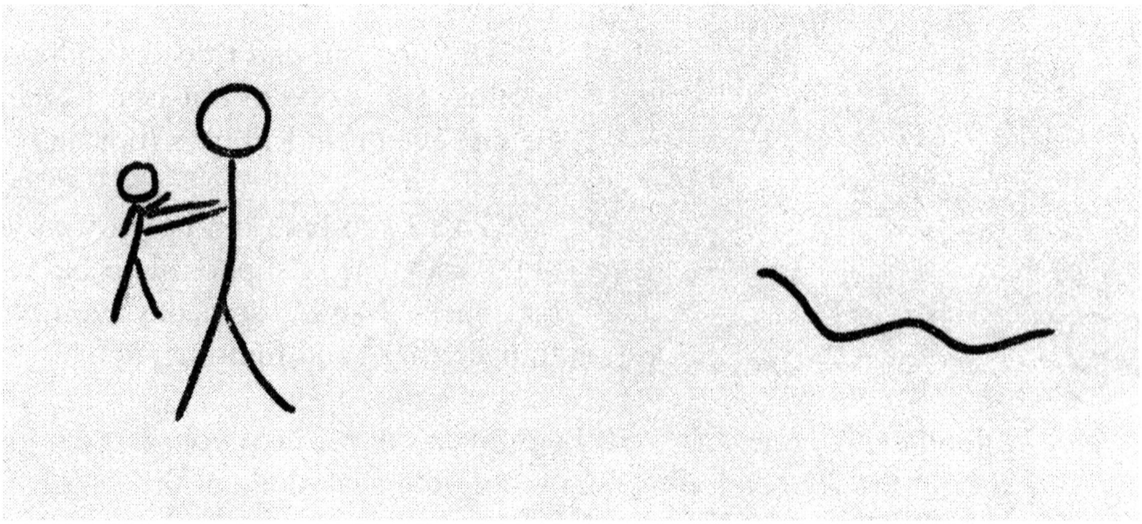

11 May 1969

Wilbur

[The pig]

I guess I must be the luckiest pig in Banaue, maybe even in all of Ifugao. Just two days ago I was brought up here to be sacrificed. And now I'm like a pet and have even been named Wilbur, after the hero of *Charlotte's Web*, except here it sounds more like Wereburr and except it is a male name and I am a female. But I don't really care, I am so happy to be safe.

Perhaps it was my good looks that did the trick. I don't like to seem conceited, but you don't have to have had a lot of experience as a county-fair judge to see for yourself. Look at these two pictures:

Wilbur, the pig.

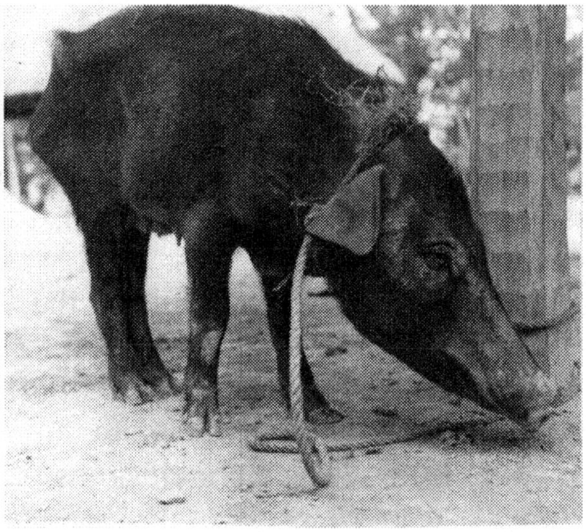

One less fortunate.

This is me on the left. The character on the right was one of the others on the jeep with me. When the father saw me he said, "Hey, look at this one. She is just about the best-looking pig I've ever seen up here."

If it wasn't my fantastic body that saved my life, it might have been my cool personality. I'm good-natured, and even though I was exhausted from the hike in from Līwang, I let the little kids lead me around on a rope. When I got tired I flopped down on the ground. The kids started to poke me and pretend that they were priests at a ritual, pretending to be piercing my heart with a sharp spike. Kids are kids all over the world. Instead of getting all panicky like other pigs would have done, and squealing and writhing around in an undignified manner, I just lay really still and closed my eyes and smiled. I guess it tickled a little. This took everyone by surprise, and everyone wanted a turn at rubbing my tummy, which suited me just fine.

Finally it was supper time, and man, was I hungry! The people were generous. Even though they were planning to kill us all in a few days, they arranged for someone to bring in a huge bundle of sweet potato vines, chop them all up into tiny shreds like cole slaw, and even to boil them up. It sure tasted good. I was famished, but I was very careful not to put my feet into the basin. The mother, naturally, was the first to notice. "Say, this pig even has good manners!"

Well, after everything quieted down for the night, I spent a lot of time rooting up the soil around the stones of the house terrace, and also around the bases of three newly planted *dongla* plants. This was a naughty thing to do especially because the *dongla* is one of the sacred plants of the Ifugao; but I just couldn't help it since, after all, I am a pig. In the morning I even tried to reach the sacred red leaves, but I was too short. So I spent time chasing the chickens. The father patted me on the head on his way to shave.

And Bruce shouted, "Īna, this pig is really funny. He thinks he owns this place and he is chasing away any animal that comes around to the dirt he dug up with his nose. Even our chickens; he is chasing away our chickens."

That kid Bruce doesn't distinguish between *he* and *she* in English anymore, but his mother should know. She said, "He is kind of cute. It is too bad we have to kill him. He acts like a pet instead of a pig. Maybe we should try to find another pig to take his place."

I heard all this as I was lying on the ground. Several people were rubbing my stomach. I thought I might be dreaming, but I opened one eye and saw that it was all true.

“Well, if you want to do that, we better act quickly. Do you want Nangleg to try to buy another pig when he goes into town?”

Puggūwon was counting my nipples and contemplating how tall I would eventually get, and offered to take care of me—then half of the piglets would be his.

“If there are any pigs left in town, it would be a good idea. It is really a pity to kill this one. He is cute.”

She keeps saying that. I guess it must be true. I *am* cute.

12 May 1969

Ritual for a new shelf

[The cat]

This is me, the cat, again. I've been busy having kittens. My second litter was born back in January. One kitten died soon after birth, one died after it was given away, but two are thriving in their new surroundings.

The present set was born about two weeks ago. They are the cutest yet—a mixture of white and orange-brown from me and gray-black from their father. I like to have my litters up in the half-attic of the cookhouse where they will be safe from the dogs. When it was time, I went around to the mother and mewed until she went over to the cookhouse with me. Then I mewed some more until she emptied a box that had rolls of rattan in it. Then I climbed in and had four kittens. To tell you the truth, the mother is pretty good with animals. The other day when Bruce was away she was the only one who was able to catch the monkey when it broke away from its tree house.

The boys kept a flashlight and one of the house ladders in the cookhouse so that they could check on us several times a day. I didn't mind when they just looked, but then they got the idea of weighing the kittens every other day. It made me nervous when they picked them up and put them on a postage scale, so I decided to move the kittens over to the attic of the field lab. Quite a job. One by one I took them by the neck, jumped down six feet, hurried to the porch, and jumped up ten feet to the attic.

Very shortly after I had gotten settled, there was a lot of chanting, foot-stomping, and gong-playing over in the house. I could also hear the men laughing and talking and arguing, as if they might be getting drunk; and I guess they were also eating on and off because I could smell chicken feathers burning and the meat stewing. Another one of those all-night rituals, this time to install a newly-carved *halada'*, the shelf inside the house for heirloom jars, baskets, and other things. As is often the case in ritual events, two birds can be killed with one stone, and since this ritual was taking place in May, it was decided to celebrate Mark's birthday as well. The mother and the boys moved their blankets to the lab and went to sleep, but the father stayed up most of the night, with earphones on his head, recording things on his tape recorder.

Preparing pigs for sacrifice.

The next day all except the little brown pig, Wilbur, were rounded up and their legs securely tied. What a terrible noise they made, and the boys had a wonderful time. Here they are, teasing Wilbur, making her think she is going to be tied up too. Everything was being recorded and Mark asked to hear how the squealing sounded on tape. The father stopped the recorder, rewound the reel-to-reel tape a bit to listen, and definitely didn't like what he heard—an impossible and unintelligible jumble of noises partly caused by a malfunctioning erase-head. As it turned out, all but two of the days' recordings had been ruined! He felt terrible and tried to explain to Puggūwon what had happened. Puggūwon is the kind of guy you can tell things to, because even if he doesn't understand, he knows how you feel.

The ritual outside went on. The pigs were slaughtered. I noticed that Wilbur stayed away until it was all over. The pigs were divided into sizeable shares for the participating priests, a special cut was put aside for the man who had carved the shelf, and the rest was divided into 18 equal shares for the family's friends.

The second night was very quiet. Everyone was exhausted. I could hear the carabao scratching his side against the wall of the lab. Poor thing. He didn't have a clue as to what was in store for him, even when they drew chalk lines all over him the next morning to show how he would be divided up.

He wasn't allowed to eat anything, but Mark asked permission to give him one last bucket of water. Even as the men led the poor critter up to the post he appeared quite oblivious of what was in the offing. Three men with extra-long, heavy bolos delivered one whack each to the neck and it was all over. At this point all resemblance to a typical Ifugao ritual ended—no shouting and arguing! Everyone sat patiently while a large spring scale was tied to a house beam and the carabao was cut into weighable hunks. Mark hung around until the head was detached, and posed proudly with it for several pictures. The head is his and, after being properly cured and dried, will hang under the eaves of our house as Mark's eighth birthday souvenir.

A formula for the distribution of meat—so that the family could be traditional and not traditional at the same time, and show favoritism and not show favoritism at the same time—was all worked out beforehand, down to the urinary bladder and tail. Receiving one of the hind quarters means a really special bond, and Mark gave one each to Bu'way and Immay. Then followed the priests' shares of good meat, equal except that the head priest got more. Then equal shares for the people who work on the project. Then equal shares for the households in the hamlet. Then the urinary bladder to one bratty kid, and the tail to another bratty kid, just because their families are important. Frankly I can't remember if you got two shares if you were a worker and also a neighbor. But, however it was decided, no one, and I say no one, complained, and that is not traditional.

21 May 1969

Termites and an all-day hike

[Mark]

There is so much to do around here, I wish I didn't have to waste time with schoolwork. Every day I have to do reading—and even worse—take-aways. No wonder I can't understand take-aways. I can hear the kids playing outside. They are just a few houses away and I can tell from the voices who are spinning their tops, and whose top got hit out of the yard and into the bushes, and who is crying, and who cares what '16, take away 9,' is anyway. Oh, oh, sounds like Kalluh's top got cracked. It was his best one I bet. The other kids are just laughing. Now they are starting another game—teams take turns throwing their tops, trying to knock the other team's tops out of line.

"What? '14, take away 5?' I did that already yesterday."

"Oh, all right, '14, take away 5.' Let's see, '14, take away 5,' '14, take away 5.' Yeah, that's easy. 8. No? Not 8? 7? 6?"

"I *am so* trying. '14, take away 5.' Is there some trick to remember this one? Not 6, not 7, not 8...9. Is it 9? 9!! Can I go now?"

Guess what I ate the other night—roasted termites! Once a year the mating forms fly out, all at the same time, to set up new colonies. The people wait near the nest openings with water in their large laundry basins and a kerosene lamp sitting in the middle of the basin. The insects are attracted to the light, and as they are darting around, their wings touch the water. With wet wings they can't fly and so they drop into the basin. Then you take large handfuls of termites and put them in a flat pan and toast them over a fire. They get crispy and a little greasy, and if you eat too many you get diarrhea. They are really good.

Catching flying termites.

One day we had a real treat. No school. I think Īna is as tired of school as I am. She said she wanted us to have a chance to hike to a particularly good swimming place before the rainy season began, and she wanted us to do it while Bangluy was still around to go along with us. We have known Bangluy a long time. He is kind of like a big brother to us because he is kind of like a younger brother to Immay, and when she used to take care of me I spent a lot of time at their house. He's leaving soon to attend automobile mechanic school in the lowlands.

Mark, Bangluy, and Bruce

We left in the morning with Bangluy, Bihtul, and Dābid, and a lot of other friends, taking our lunch of rice and canned sardines. Īna forgot to pack a canteen of water and worried about me all day, but it didn't matter because I was having so much fun, and we found a place along the trail where the water comes out from between the rocks.

Īwo', our destination, is several kilometers beyond Kinnākin, in Gīlut. It was a large deep pool. We measured its depth by tying a rock to a vine and then letting it down until it touched the bottom. Maybe it was 40 feet (or maybe the current pushed the rock downstream so that it didn't go straight down). There was a kind of waterfall at one end where we could slide down over the rocks into the water. There were some other kids there, but they weren't mean, and they didn't stare at our you-know-whats like the kids do at our local swimming place. That's why I don't usually go swimming with Bruce and the other kids. I hate it when they make fun of me, and I don't like to play water tag either because the kids are too rough, and I am always 'it' because I can't catch anyone.

But today I really had a fun time. Using our slingshots, we caught some fish and roasted them under the coals. On the way home we saw a colorful wild chicken, and also the carabao that Ekka's father owns and that he is allowing to graze on a grassy hillside away from peoples' fields. While we rested near the drinking place, Bihtul made us some little bamboo flutes with three finger-holes. After that we felt refreshed and ran along the flat stretches playing our flutes. It was better than take-aways.

Swimming at Īwo'.

26 May 1969

More of the truth

[Jean]

Hal has just returned from a week-long trek through an area far to the east of here. The crew included Puggūwon (far right) to do the mapping, Bu'way (holding large circular hat) to help record texts and take notes, old Omehang (holding spear) as guide because he had been through the region before, and Dangpah (buttoning shirt) to help carry the gear. They look exhausted and hot and glad to be back home.

Hal and crew, glad to be home again.

Traveling outside of one's home territory is always a little stressful. One never knows if someone will use the opportunity to take revenge for a past killing. The whole crew was uneasy, though not as much as when they accompanied Hal on a previous trip to the south. A long time ago, a group from that region raided the Kinnākin to Banaue area. The people from "our side" fought back and killed them all. They say that the streams turned red with blood, and a large number of the skulls displayed under local eaves today are souvenirs of that battle.

Fortunately, this trip was a peaceful one. They visited an old potter who promised to come to Baynīnan some day to demonstrate his work, and they visited Roy Franklin Barton's Ifugao wife. Domengga was pleased to see Hal and to look at some of the photographs that Barton (teacher/anthropologist) had taken of her in 1916. When the visit was over, she insisted on giving Hal a chicken (in the container in Hal's hand, see photo), the customary gift for a young relative on a first visit to your home.

Bruce and Mark at school.

As for Bruce and Mark, things are good and bad. They—and I—are getting bored with the daily school sessions. Bruce is currently stuck on the 7 times's though he caught on to long division right away. Mark does the work, grudgingly going through the necessary steps, but he doesn't seem to understand what he is doing. If he gets the right answer, it's just luck.

When out of school they are competitive and fight with each other frequently. One solution to this has been to separate them by having a morning session for one and an afternoon session for the other. My fieldwork time is more broken up, but many of the tasks I've been working on are so tedious that this may be a good thing.

What kind of work do I do? Other than routine chores like keeping a diary, typing letters, filing, helping alphabetize slips by the thousands, sorting and dating photographs, ordering supplies, recording expenses, making out travel vouchers, and keeping the Coleman lanterns in repair, here are some examples:

a) Adding the Philippine National Museum's scientific identifications to the native plant type file. A half-inch of slips takes all day, and the file is 16 inches thick.

b) Typing the place name list, complete with the most complex tabbing and letter code ever devised, to tell you everything you ever wanted to know about a particular name—e.g., is/was the name a hamlet, a field, a test field, or a spirit, and if it was ever referred to in the literature.

c) Organizing the animal name file, transferring the specimen field numbers and the Philippine National Museum identifications to the appropriate slip, and then typing the whole list.

d) Graphing temperature and rain records collected from various locations.

e) Trying to determine the month the five-year-old hygrothermograph died of old age by comparing numerous records.

I also have a role here as medicine dispenser, but it is minimal. If someone seems seriously ill, relatives hold their own curing ritual; and if the patient doesn't improve, he is taken to one of the missionary clinics in Banaue. I limit myself to treatment of occasional headaches, the common cold, coughs due to colds, simple wounds, and worms.

I am assuming that everyone, including us, has worms, and every few months I organize an intensive distribution of worm medicine. The results are often spectacular, especially among the neighboring children. One of the mothers asked me how her child could have so many (36; she counted them!), so I seized the opportunity to explain to her and to those listening how children re-infest themselves and how it is a good idea to wash one's hands before eating. The mother smiled one of those how-interesting-but-it-won't-work smiles and told me that she has tried to get her son to wash his hands, but he won't. And when she speaks sharply to him, he whacks her with his bolo.

I will digress a moment here to say that while I think their system of child rearing too permissive, they consider me too strict. Once after I had bragged a little that Bruce and Mark were getting better about obeying me, a mother commented, "They are afraid of you." Little children have been known to run away when they see me.

And another time Mark was playing alone, pretending soldier with our surplus army field supplies. He stationed himself outside the lab door and stood at attention like a guard for a long time, hoping that I would come out and notice him there. Later he told me that the people thought he was being punished for something.

The other topic I have given up mentioning is birth control. With inheritance patterns that favor the first born, even they can see that it is not enviable to be the youngest child of a youngest child. Nevertheless, the more relatives an Ifugao has the more secure he feels, and coming from a large family or having a large family is something to be proud of. It is so important to have a child to whom one can pass on fields that an unproductive marriage is considered reason enough for a divorce. I have often wondered if the pressure that a couple, especially a wealthy one, may feel to produce has anything to do with the high number of childless marriages noted among those who own large fields. These marriages, and who will get what if a couple remains childless, are much discussed. I understand that adoption is not a guaranteed solution. Even if adoptive parents want their fields to pass on to an adopted child, they face an often-lost battle with blood relatives.

To get back to my role as medicine dispenser, I have two special patients. One is an old, old man, Bad'i (pyud-'ee), with a very wrinkled weathered face. Every once in a while he hikes down to our place, and since he is the *only* person who ever comes by just to ask for me, I make a special effort to see him no matter what I happen to be doing. Then our little comedy begins. He beams his toothless smile and starts talking, repeatedly pulling his hands over his face. Then I smile and answer. Then he smiles and answers. Neither one understands a word of what the other is saying, except that I know he has run out of the medicine that makes his face stop itching, and he knows that I have another tube for him. It's one of those things that should have been taped.

Bad'i

Ottēngan

My other patient is Ottengan, the ritual head of the community. We have a sort of unspoken agreement. He takes care of our ritual needs and we supply him with medicine for his asthma attacks and coughing spells. (Within the community he takes care of their ritual needs and they supply him with *bayah* and ritual meat.) Although I have tried to explain to him that the asthma pills will lose their effectiveness if taken too often, he runs through a month's supply in a week and seems really hooked! I could give him the pills one at a time (he would love the attention) but I don't have the time or patience. So my job is one of guessing whether he is having a genuine attack (then he gets something from the asthma box) or if he's faking, hanging over the back of his bench, gasping and spitting for attention (then he gets an aspirin or a vitamin pill).

Our own health has been good except for occasional colds or mysterious fevers, but these run their course and go away. Bruce had one miserable week—headache, sore throat, fever; plus enlarged lymph nodes associated with an infected foot; and a swollen and itchy penis. I applied a mixture of four ointments to the latter hoping that one would be effective, and finally the irritation went away.

I guess *my* worst week was when my left knee swelled up so badly that I couldn't bend my leg. An excellent excuse for not having to hike, but it turned a trip to the outhouse into a major acrobatic feat.

Insects seem to zero in on Mark. Insect repellent probably helps but still he is covered with bites in every stage—new-itchy bites, open-bleeding-from-scratching bites, infected bites, scabs, and scars. He is much too busy having a good time to worry about his appearance. In the middle of one exuberant play session Mark ran past me and shouted, *hey pohdo' ya 'adi' maliwwan 'an munhāpet hi 'inglih 'unna' mun'ay'ayyam hidid maleka* (I hope I will remember to speak in English when I am playing in America).

Except for occasional quiet moments the boys have thrown themselves into the community. When a local house was dismantled and moved they joined the others in the treasure hunt for discarded objects—nails, loom parts, broken baskets, and empty tin cans. Bruce roams the woods nearby, climbs trees, makes spear guns from bamboo, and roughhouses with the others at the river.

Mark celebrated the end of a one-month-of-no-gong-playing penalty (the most severe punishment that we could think of for biting Hal; actually I can't remember why he bit him) by rising at dawn and beating out all the rhythms he knew. He seems to have the ear and necessary coordination for playing the gongs and is the only Conklin who can do it.

As I look at this photo I think maybe our solution to the food problem was inadequate. Mark is so thin. I've decided to import supplies from Baguio. Our garden was a giant failure because it got planted with only beans and onions and these were planted all at the same time instead of being staggered. We ended up having beans and onions for a week and giving basketloads away to all the neighbors.

Mark practicing gong beating under our house.

15 June 1969

The boiling water ordeal

[Bruce]

What I really like best is spinning *bawwot* (tops) and I'm getting to be pretty good at it. But I can't make them yet. Fortunately Mark and I have friends who are nice enough to carve them for us—and sometimes generous enough to give us really good ones—you know, shaped just right for the size, and balanced, and made out of the best wood.

Boys playing with wooden tops.

There is a certain kind of hardwood tree, *gale''on*, the roots of which provide the best quality, tough-grained wood for tops. One night a large *gale''on* fell over in a nearby forest leaving the roots exposed. All the kids were planning to go over to get a supply. I explained this to Īna and told her how Kalluh had promised us a good piece (it was in his family's forest), and I asked if we could go so we could see what this tree looked like and find out more about it. She said OK—and canceled school! That's the trick. She's satisfied as long as we are *learning* something.

Well, one day last week I *really* learned something. Mark, Kalluh (kahl-loos), and I were shooting small stones out of the "school" window with our slingshots. We could see that runny-nosed whiny pest Ekka playing down in the woods so we decided to tease her by shooting in her direction. By accident I hit her right on the forehead between her eyes. Naturally she started to scream, and her visiting cousin who was baby-sitting began crying and blabbering that I had done it on purpose. Kalluh took off, and Mark and I were left to decide what we should do.

Well, Ekka's cousin complained all day, but she was only twelve so no one paid much attention. However, when Ekka's mother came home from the fields she really exploded. She's one of those types that doesn't like to get pushed around, and since she married into an important family in this neighborhood, everyone listens when she explodes.

When my mother asked me if I did it, I said, "No." She believed me and this made me feel worse. Meanwhile Ekka's mother yelled louder and louder and began to threaten all kinds of things because naturally she believed Ekka; and all the while everyone could see that one of Ekka's eyes was quite swollen and even getting black! Mark and I decided on a "play-as-usual" plan, and we went out of our way to look as if we were having a good time.

Finally, my father became concerned because even if I hadn't done it, it wouldn't be good if the others thought I might have. So he and Puggūwon talked it over and finally called me in.

As you can imagine, by this time I was really feeling terrible because it was getting harder and harder to say I hadn't done it, and at the same time harder and harder to say I *had* done it! I really didn't know what to do. Maybe it would have blown over after Ekka's eye got better, but my father thought it would be best to have it definitely settled. He and Puggūwon suggested that one way would be by *dau*, the boiling water ordeal. Although this was discussed in Ifugao they didn't have to explain it to me because I had already heard a lot about these tests. They would put an egg into a pot of boiling water and all possible suspects (everyone with a slingshot, including me) would have to reach in and try to get the egg. There would be all my friends, and me, and Markie. Only the guilty one would get burned. My whole body was sweating just thinking about it. What a mess to be in. Finally I decided to tell them the truth no matter what happened. Already I felt a little better.

My father, mother, Puggūwon, and his wife talked it over and discussed various elaborate possibilities to smooth things over—maybe a ritual, or payment in pigs, or chickens, or all three. But finally it was decided that it might be best for me to go to Ekka's house directly and to tell her I did it.

Ten-year-old Bruce.

It wasn't easy but still I was glad to get it over with. I can't remember what I said. I was so upset that afterwards I came home and threw up. Through Puggūwon, my father offered to pay a fine to Ekka's family, but Ekka's mother said, "Never mind, we are all relatives and I would feel embarrassed. Anyway it was just a child playing."

Kalluh sure was loyal that day. He didn't tell even though Ekka was a close relative. He is a good friend, and in fact Mark and I have lots of friends. Sometimes we fight, then it's over and the next day we play.

5 August 1969

The wildcat attacks

[The cat]

Can you imagine what it would be like if one night a gorilla walked into your home and tried to take your children away? Well, it was like that for me. Compared to me the gray *tābo* (male wildcat) is like a gorilla. He has become so bold lately, prowling close to our hamlet even before dark. When the present set of kittens was about 12-weeks-old (by that time there were only three), it seemed to me he was trying to kidnap them. Even if he is their father, he is no good, so I tried to protect them by moving them to the attic of the field laboratory. I figured a wildcat wouldn't dare try anything as long as the lamp was going. But the father complained because I stepped on his 4 x 6 slips when I jumped down from the attic, so the mother moved us back to the kitchen.

Well, one evening the *tābo* came into the cookhouse, right in under the eaves, the way I get in and out. I put up a terrible fight, and we made such a racket that everyone came over to see what was going on. By the time they opened the door he had gone and I was licking my wounds, and they went away thinking it was just a domestic argument.

Later that night after everyone had gone to sleep, he returned. This time it was a battle. I was badly scratched and my tongue and lip were ripped. I managed to drive him away, but in the end one kitten was dead, and the other two were missing. I was in a state of shock and wouldn't let anyone come near me.

The next morning the boys buried the little gray kitten. Everyone was restless. The boys couldn't concentrate on their schoolwork, and the mother couldn't teach. I roamed around the cookhouse whining and sniffing, which gave Puggūwon an idea. He rolled up the reed flooring. There, huddled in a tiny space, was one of the missing kittens—his voice hoarse and his neck wounded, but he was alive.

You'll never believe it, but the next day the third kitten was found in a small cave at the bottom of the hill. One of the boys in the hamlet happened to be passing by and heard it mewing. He brought it back and the family promised it to him as soon as it was stronger and old enough to leave me.

Except for this, things are going very well. After months and months of rain we all appreciated the dry season with warmer days and warmer nights. During this time of year there were more visitors too. Jon and Judy Kress took some time from his archaeological work in the southern Philippines to visit for a few days. Mark acted as their guide around the village and even took them down to the river because Bruce's foot was infected. Mark usually stays away from the river, but he felt safe with Jon who happens to know judo. In addition, the attention that Mark thinks is focused on his circumcision was diverted to the visitors—one hairy (body hair is considered freaky, even revolting) and the other in bikini underwear.

Bruce and Kalluh helping to carry in harvested rice.

By lucky coincidence, right in the middle of this visit, along came the old potter with a supply of clay with which to demonstrate his skills. He set to work and everyone took pictures. After a pot had been shaped, he placed it in the sun and went with the others for a chew of betel and a drink of *bayah.* And do you know what that stupid Wilbur did? Wilbur went up to the pot and tried to eat it. Before anyone could stop her it was bent out of shape. Although the potter did his best to straighten it out, he wasn't entirely successful.

Wilbur is really a nuisance. She doesn't seem to realize that she is a pig. She tries repeatedly to get into the cookhouse when the family is eating. During the rice harvest they had to pen her up to keep her from eating the rice bundles that were drying in the sun.

Everyone is psyched up for harvesting. Mark and Bruce have their own carrying poles and helped to bring in the first bundles. After a couple of trips though, they had to give up. You know I can hardly tell those two from the rest of the kids anymore. They are into everything and most of the time they are even dirtier than the rest. It seems as though they are trying to cram a whole year of playing into a few weeks. They took out a few minutes to participate in their official name-changing hair-cutting ritual. Nothing spectacular, just another excuse for sacrificing a few pigs and drinking *bayah*.

Bandaw giving Bruce a ritual haircut.

There's something different in the air though—a kind of frenzied attempt by everyone who is working on something to get finished. Things are getting sorted, listed, and packed. The boys' books, all the *National Geographic*s, and extra school supplies were carried over to the Kinnākin Elementary School. Standard medicines and food supplies were divided up and given away. Special medicines went to the clinic, and non-Ifugao type foods went to Mr. Hester, the nice old gentleman who built his summer home in Banaue. Even blankets and sheets were sorted out and the names of the next owners attached.

The father gave away some of his shirts, but the rest of his clothes are too big to be of use to anyone here. The mother had only a sweater and some blouses to give away because she has worn Ifugao skirts that have no special local value. Almost all the boys' things went to their friends, and a couple of days ago I thought I had blown my mind. The kids were playing around and everyone was wearing something that belonged to Mark or Bruce—or now I should say Bumanghat and Bindādan (poo-mahng-haht and peen-CHA-chan).

8 August 1969

Time runs out

[Jean]

As the number of remaining field hours dwindled, Hal's activities became more frantic. Too many projects were coming along, but not quite finished. If it weren't necessary to return to New Haven in time for the beginning of the fall term, he would have been delighted to stay on—and on.

As always, the final days were hectic. Puggūwon's work on the maps was essential, so I did more and more of the cooking. When lamplighting time rolled around I looked up from one of my interminable tasks and realized that what everyone else was doing was important and that they were expecting me to light the blasted Colemans. All my spare minutes have been tied up sorting research supplies, books, food, clothing, and medicines, and making lists of what we were taking, what we were leaving, and what we were giving away and to whom. This particular job suits me well since I am by nature a sorter and list maker, and enjoy getting rid of things.

Hal has been comfortable and contented in the field, completely absorbed in documenting as much about everything as possible. The crew is devoted to him. They, seemingly effortlessly, always cheerfully, are able to keep up with his demand for detail and accuracy and long work hours. Community members accept him wholeheartedly; they enjoy his company as much as he enjoys theirs.

Bruce and Mark have lived a full life here. After we officially stopped our school sessions a month or so ago, they spontaneously joined into any activity appropriate for their ages. And it was often through them that we became aware that something important was going on. Once a drunken argument was threatening to develop into armed combat. Another time a large quantity of earth was being moved by a rarely used technique. Once it was a dead dog about to be cooked for a snack. We then had a choice: grab a notebook or camera and go, or have a detailed description later.

There were many moments this year when I would have gladly packed up and gone home. But at every stage it was clear that the boys were gaining more from the experience than I was losing, so we were all here as the last bundles of rice were harvested, sun-dried, and put into storage. Bruce joined the group of boys in a post-harvest ritual of planting *dongla* (*Cordyline fruticos* (L.) A. Chev. [*C. terminalis* Kunth.] PNH 72890, 72891, field no. 564, 565; sorry about that, I'm so well trained now) leaves at the river boundary between Baynīnan and Kinnākin. Mark, self-appointed guide to Georges Condominas, our last guest, followed the group as they chanted and danced their way along the terraces, but stopped at a comfortable distance just in case Kinnākin decided to dispute the border marker.

Finally everything was in order. As I sat checking the pay envelopes, the cat walked into the lab, jumped up on the desk, and started rubbing her face against my arms, chest, and face. It was as if she knew this departure was different from the three short trips we had taken during the year. She was saying, "Good-bye, I'm going to miss you," and I knew I was going to miss her too.

After the last carton was taken up to Līwang I went around to see neighbors for the last time. Close friends hiked up to the end of the trail with us. It was drizzly and slippery, and as always, I was struggling to keep on my feet and was the last to reach the road where the truck was being loaded. The atmosphere was depressing; the drizzle continued, no one laughed, no one cried, no one could think of anything to say. Mark saved the day by doing a few of his hilarious imitations before the last rope was secured and we were off. The four of us spoke little during our ride into Banaue. It was hard to believe that this was truly the end of an unusual experience.

April 2002

Epilogue

It is now thirtysomething years later. The Baynīnan settlements are far enough off the main road to still be without electricity and running water. Maintenance of the *payo*, the cultivation of rice, and growing of sweet potatoes and vegetables in the hillside swiddens and gardens remain the primary focus of the people. Yet the world has expanded for many residents. If they themselves have not gone to school beyond high school or taken a job abroad as a governess or hotel or hospital worker, someone in their immediate family or a close relative has. Hong Kong, Saudi Arabia, Canada, and the States are popular destinations. Even so, Ifugao is still considered to be their home and they return for major events, funerals and reburials, weddings, and if possible, even harvests.

Puggūwon is still taking care of our house and associated structures, and he continues to provide drawings of pond fields and sketches of community events. He and Malīngay had a number of children and have become grandparents several times over. Two of his children have become valued research assistants.

Two of Bu'way's children married Peace Corp volunteers and now live in the States. Bu'way still works on linguistic materials, on his own as well as when Hal is in residence.

Ottēngan died in 1983. He has passed on his ritual field, along with the obligatory agricultural decision-making, to his older daughter. Having no natural child of her own, she has now given it to her nephew, Ālen, one of Bruce's and Mark's playmates in 1968-69. Ālen's older brother, Kalluh, has moved away.

Wilbur the pig turned out to be a lousy mother, got sick, and had to be sacrificed. On the other hand, the cat remained active for many years after our departure. She may well have been our greatest contribution to the community.

Thanks to her and her progeny, it is said that Baynīnan fields suffered less in rice damage from rats than neighboring areas.

As for the bratty, runny-nosed, insect-bitten kids in the narrative, they turned out all right in the end. Bruce and Mark readjusted quickly and completely to life in New Haven. Bruce found an after-school job taking care of exotic animals and happily accepted a Burmese python as pay for his work. Mark finally caught on to subtraction, became the official school drummer, and starred in many school plays. Both feel that their years in the field played an important part in shaping their outlook on life.

Bruce's interest in animals and biology led him to medical school. He is now a medical researcher in San Francisco. And it should be no surprise that Mark worked as an actor in New York City for fifteen years. He moved recently to Utah where he has entered the world of software management and information technology.

Both boys have returned to Baynīnan for short visits—Bruce in 1980, then again in 1990 with his wife, Bonnie, and most recently, in the summer of 2001, with Bonnie and the children, nine-year-old Dylan and six-year-old Claire. Their visit was celebrated with the sacrifice of five pigs and a generous supply of rice beer for research assistants and families, neighbors, and friends. Dylan was given the name Bihtul; and Claire is Būgan.

Mark made a return visit in 1990, and again in 1995 with his wife, Noelle. On this occasion, as well as when Bruce and Bonnie visited in 1990, Hal arranged traditional Ifugao celebrations with the killing of sacrificial pigs and chickens, drinking of rice beer, dancing, and chanting and calling to the ancestors of both families to bestow good fortune to the couples.

Each return trip has included a reunion with Immay who had taken care of the boys in 1962–63. Immay is regarded by us and by the community as a member of our family. She married, had several children, and has continued to help Hal by sharing her special knowledge of weaving and rice seed selection, among other things. Our friends in Baynīnan were delighted to learn that Mark's recently-born daughter had been named Emma, because they assumed "Emma" was an American version of "Immay".

As for myself, I returned to Baynīnan for a short visit in 1983. It was lovely to see friends and neighbors again, but the trails remain as slippery as ever and my legs aren't up to the challenge of another trip.

To all friends and neighbors in Baynīnan, past and present, I wish to express my gratitude for all that you did, and are currently doing, for my family.

Immay and Mark, 1962

Appendix A

"Ten Things I Like Here"

The following lists of "Ten things I like here" were composed on the spur of the moment. No one spent more than 15 minutes making his list. Although additions and substitutions were thought of later, the original items are listed here.

3 May 1969

Ten things I like here

[Mark]

1. more friends than you usually have in the States
2. more places to walk
3. don't have to watch out for cars and things
4. riding the carabao
5. shooting my slingshot
6. playing in the mud
7. fighting, teasing, spitting, kicking, and biting
8. climbing trees
9. chewing betel
10. pretending to kill *nuwang* (carabao)
11. pretending to *mun'ihāwa* (teasing girls about making out with them)
12. Puggūwon (cartographer, kitchen helper, friend)
13. Kalluh (friend)

Mark, with friends,

with his carabao,

and with Hūwan of Ballang.

3 May 1969

Ten things I like here

[Bruce]

1. *palhē'et* (slingshot)
2. Kalluh (friend)
3. Dunyul (friend)
4. *mun'u'uwādi* (animals)
5. the cat
6. the *bullang* (monkey, what else!)
7. spears
8. going to the river
9. pancakes
10. Puggūwon (cartographer, kitchen helper, friend)

Joining dancers at a mock headhunting ritual.

26 May 1969

Ten things I like here

[Jean]

1. misty nights with the houses, trees, and mountains silhouetted
2. the fireplace
3. Immay (cared for the boys during previous field trip)
4. giving out medicine and having people get better
5. watching Bruce and Mark having a good time
6. feeling clean after washing my hair and taking a bath
7. the cat, monkey, and Wilbur
8. a few other people
9. learning something new like how to tell if a pair of shorts are going to fit (if they will go around your neck, they will fit because neck measurements are approximately half waist measurements)
10. reading outdated *Newsweek*s from cover to cover

Bruce and Mark at doorway of our house.

Carabao made of banana stem and sticks.

String figures.

At hearth in our house.

12 June 1969

Ten things I like here

[Hal]

1. Puggūwon's versatility with paper and pencil (mapping and drawing) and in quietly managing our Baynīnan logistics
2. Bu'way's patience and language virtuosity
3. Malīngay's natural beauty
4. Immay's sparkle when watching Markie
5. conversations with characters such as Ammeng, Maggūway, Gonggong, Hūwan (of Ballang), Hūwan (of Bīnong)
6. kids like Duddūli (chood-CHOO-lee), Dābid, Pēlek, Ālen
7. Dol'am's (chore-'ahm) fine craftsmanship
8. view from our *duhku* (lookout) of the falls at Am'al, with the peak of Mt. Inulītan in the mist
9. view toward the southeast in early morning, from the irrigation canal
10. *buble* (our hamlet) in the moonlight, from Bullud or our *'ābung* (field lab)

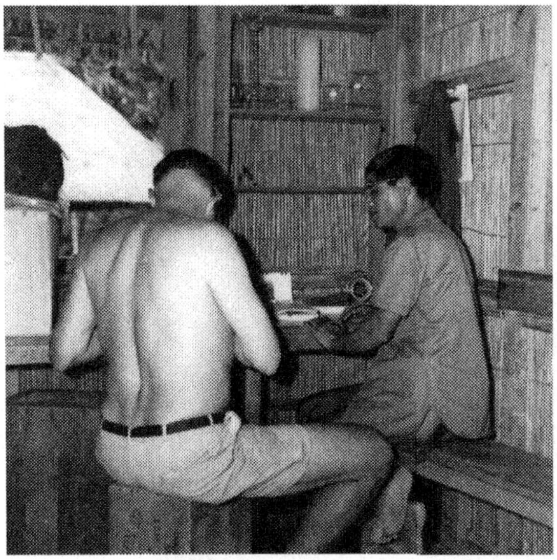

Hal, Bu'way

Duddūli, Gonggong

Am'al Falls

Puggūwon's wife, Malīngay

Duddūli, Bandaw, Kaleng; Gonggong in background

Hal and Puggūwon

Appendix B

Boys' Compositions

The school curriculum for Bruce and Mark during the year was a combination of material from the Calvert School, one of several correspondence schools used by Americans living overseas, and from their school in New Haven. Whenever a composition was required, I encouraged them to choose a theme from their field experience. A sampling is included here.

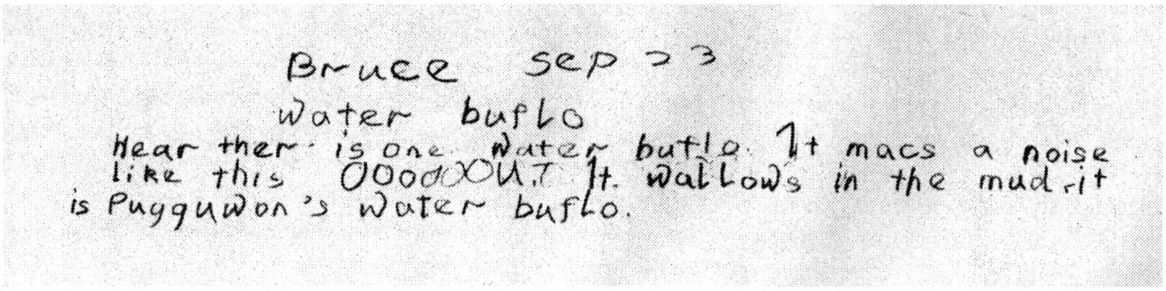

Bruce sep 23

water buflo

Hear ther is one water buflo. It macs a noise like this OOOdOOUT It wallows in the mud. it is Pugguwon's water buflo.

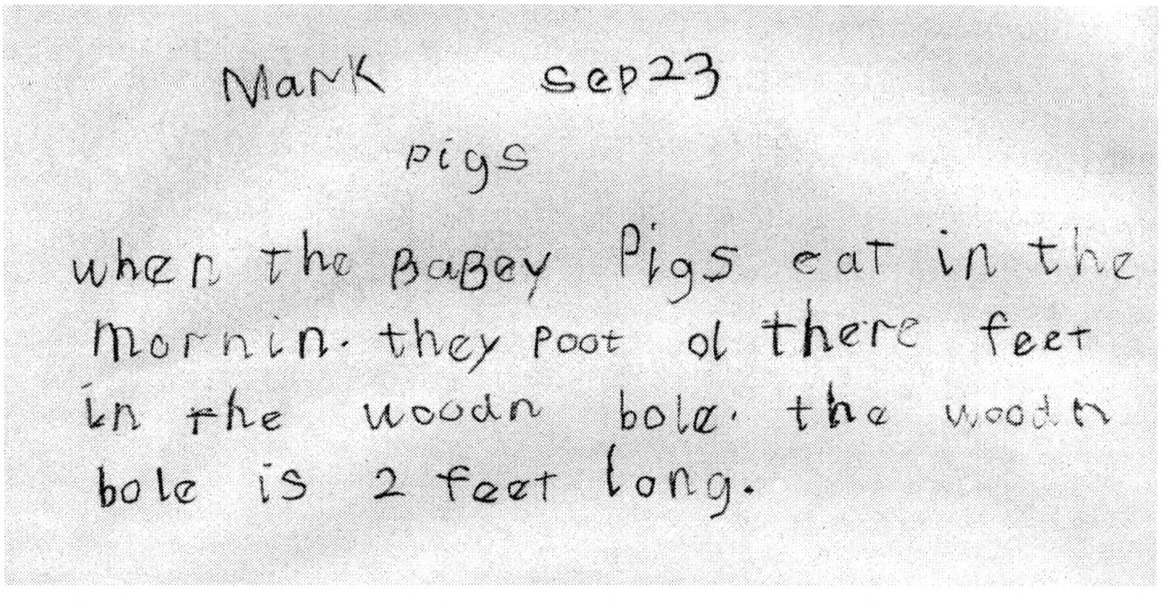

Mark sep23

pigs

when the Babey Pigs eat in the mornin. they Poot ol there feet in the woodn bole. the woodn bole is 2 feet long.

Oct. 12 Bruce
It's a long way to Kinakin.
There was a ritual in Kinakin
In Kinakin they killed a cow.
It didn't take long. They only took
two chops and he was killed. the
trail wasn't easy it was hot and
steap. To the river it was down.
but once across the bridge it
was up up up finlly down. At last
we got there.

oct.12 Mark
Yesterday in Kinna Kin. they play
d gong&fun b7 people dants. But the
dants was not the cieend of
dants I was expeeting. I liked going
bak becus we waded across therive

A Walk to See an Old, Old Friend

[Mark]

One day my father said we would all take a walk. We went over rice fields, jumped over a stream, and climbed up a steep hill. When we got there, we saw her sitting on a chair. This is how she looked.

Bu'way's mother, Addunglay, in a death chair.

"A Good Helper

I like to help Gotia feed the pigs. She lets me squash up the wormy and left-over potatoes then I call, "Kokōooo kokoooooooooo!!" and they come running. If I don't hurry and pour the food in the trough they will start biting me.

My Carabao

[Mark]

One day someone brought my carabao. He was big and nice. He liked to be rode on. Once 5 boys rode on him at one time.

We gave him a bath every day in the river, or splashed him with water. We brot him grass to eat and water to drink. One time he drank 5 buckets!!!

On the last day we took pictures of him. I gave him some water then the time came to kill him. I felt a little sad when I saw it dead.

Bad News

Yesterday we heard that two men were going to wrestle in the river. I waited all day to see it. But after we got there, all they did was throw one egg and a couple pieces of bilau. One man was hit so they said, "No more fighting."

Mark Conklin 2/17/69

Fun in Bayinan

[Mark]

Almost all the time lots of kids play together. Sometimes we hunt for birds to shoot with our *palheet*. Sometimes we us shovels and buckets to make dams. Then we go to the *payo* and catch *yuyu*. Then we end up taking off our clothes and wallowing in the mud.

Someone I Admire

[Bruce]

I Admire a man that helps us in many ways. He cooks, helps with maps, and is very strong. We like to compare him to the strongest man on earth. And also he has bin around. He used to go to the sea shore to catch squid and eat them raw. He's smart and nice and draws very well.

February 11, 1969

Dear Mrs. Burns,

This year I am in another country. Our house in the mountains has no electricity and no running water. The weather is sometimes warm and sunny, and sometimes cold and rainy.

I like animals very, very much. And my name is Bruce. Also I like to walk to the woods and walk to the river to swim and play.

I like it here because I am a boy who likes to run and play, hike and find things. In school I like reading and I hate writing. That why my letter is not very good.

Sincerely yours,

Bruce R. Conklin

The dog I'm not going to have.

Thiz iz a true story. When the pups were born, they could not see. Now they walk. But the brown dog I want died because he did not eat much.

Mark Conklin

My Little Monkey

My monkey lives in a little native house. He can walk on poles between trees, climb on branches, and swing on his chain

But I am sorry to say the children often tease him. When they do this, he jumps down and tries to catch and scratch them. Sometimes he is successful.

However I dont tease him. I give him food he likes, like buggy corn and finely powdered rice shells. Its surprising that he doesnt like bananas as much as the other things.

Appendix C

Glossary and Pronunciation Guide

'ābung	'AH-poong	non-raised house structure; our field lab
Addunglay	'ahd-chung-leigh	Bu'way's mother
Ālen	'AH-len	one of Ottēngan's grandsons
Āma	'AH-mah	father
Ammeng	'ahm-meng	Immay's aunt
Bad'i	pyud-'ee	M, one of Baynīnan elders
Baguio	BAHG-yoh	summer capital of Philippines
Ballang	pyal-lahng	one of Baynīnan settlements
Banaue	ba-NAH-wee	largest town in north-central Ifugao, popular tourist destination, market place
Bandaw	pyen-djau	Ottēngan's younger brother; also name of young boy in Baynīnan
Bangluy	pyahng-loy	M, teenager, Immay's cousin
Barton, R.F.		teacher/anthropologist in early 1900's
bawwot	pyau-wought	wooden spinning top
bayah	pya-yahh	rice beer
Baynīnan	pyay-NEE-nahn	agricultural district, our field site

Bihtul	piece-tour	M, teenager
bilāu	bee-LAH-oo	cane grass
Bindādan	peen-CHA-chan	Bruce's Ifugao name
Bīnong	PEE-nong	next hamlet below us
bolo		long bush knife
Buble	poob-lay	main settlement in agricultural district; our hamlet
Būgan	POO-kyahn	F, language assistant
bullang	pul-lahng	monkey
Bullud	pul-lood	next hamlet above us
Bumanghat	poo-mahng-haht	Mark's Ifugao name
Bu'way	poo'-wai	M, language assistant
carabao		Asian water buffalo
Dābid	CHAH-peed (fr. David)	M, teenager
Dangpah	chahng-pah	M, general helper
dau	cha-ooh	boiling water test to determine guilt
Dol'am	chore-'ahm	Ottēngan's son-in-law, carver extraordinaire
dolog	cho-logh	mudfish
Domengga	cho-meng-kyah	R.F.Barton's Ifugao wife
dongla	chong-la	red-leafed plant
Duddūli	chood-CHOO-lee	Gonggong's daughter
duhku	choohh-koo	kiosk, lookout

Dunyul	choon-yore (fr. Junior)	M, one of B/M's playmates
Ekka	'eck-kah	Kohemmay's daughter
gale''on	kyah-lay'-'ohn	hardwood tree
Gīlut	KYEE-loot	agricultural district near Baynīnan
Gonggong	kong-kong	Ottēngan's youngest sister
Gotya	kot-yah	Puggūwon's mother-in-law
halada'	hah-lah-chah'	carved shelf in Ifugao house for heirloom porcelain jars
Hūwan	HOO-wan	M, owner of largest field in Baynīnan
Ifugao	ee-foo-GAO	province in Northern Luzon
Immay	'im-mai	Mark's baby-sitter in 1962-63
Īna	'EE-nah	mother
'ingngi	'eeng-ngee	female toddler
Īwo'	'EE-woe'	place name in Gīlut
Kaleng	kah-leng	young girl in Baynīnan
kallat	kahl-laht	rubber band
Kalluh	kahl-loos (fr. Carlos)	one of Ottēngan's grandsons
Kinnākin	keen-NAH-keen	neighboring district to east
Kohemmay	koh-hem-mai	F, neighbor
la''ay	lah'-'eye	male toddler
Līwang	LEE-wahng	place on road where trail leads in to Buble
Maggūway	mag-GOO-wai	F, neighbor

Malīngay	mah-LEE-ngai	Puggūwon's wife
mun'u'uwādi	mun-'uh-'uh-WAH-chee	animal
Nangleg	nahng-leg	M, general helper
Nehtol	nehs-tore (fr. Nestor)	one of boys in Baynīnan
nuwang	noo-wahng	see carabao
Omehang	'oh-may-hahng	M, mail carrier in 1962-63
Ottēngan	'oat-TEH-ngan	Baynīnan ritual head
palhē'et	par-HAY-'et	slingshot
payo	pah-yo	see pond field
Pēlek	BAY-leck (fr. Felix)	one of boys in Baynīnan
pond field		a multi-purpose rice terrace consisting of a permanent, bunded, inundated, agricultural plot in which the main staple plus other crops are cultivated and various forms of edible fauna abound; the most valuable type of property in Ifugao
Puggūwon	poog-GOO-woan	M, mapmaker, cook, jack-of-all-trades
swidden		a temporary agricultural plot produced by cutting back and burning off vegetative cover
tābo	TAH-pooh	wildcat
Yūbel	YOO-bayr (fr. Hubert)	one of boys in Baynīnan
yūyu	YOU-you	a kind of pond-field fish

ABOUT THE AUTHOR

Jean M. Conklin is an indefatigable record keeper and avid letter writer. Both talents proved useful when she accompanied her husband, anthropologist Harold C. Conklin, on several year-long field trips to the Philippines. In addition to serving as a general assistant and keeping up with the typing, filing, and correspondence, she home-schooled their two sons during one year in the field. To help the boys, then ages seven and nine, remember their experiences and friends, she turned the details of that 1968-69 field stay into a narrative for them. *An Ifugao Notebook* is her first, and very likely last, book. She can be reached at jeanconklin@snet.net.

CPSIA information can be obtained
at www.ICGtesting.com
Printed in the USA
BVOW10s0233260516
449365BV00005B/20/P

9 781403 349170